SAME DIFFERENCE

DEREK KIRK KIM

:01

First Second

New York & London

First Second

Text and illustrations copyright © 2011 by Derek Kirk Kim
First published in *Same Difference & Other Stories* in 2004 by Top Shelf Productions.

Published by First Second
First Second is an imprint of Roaring Brook Press,
a division of Holtzbrinck Publishing Holdings Limited Partnership
175 Fifth Avenue, New York, New York 10010

I DON'T WANNA GROW UP
Written by Tom Waits and Kathleen Brennan
© JALMA MUSIC (ASCAP)
Used By Permission. All Rights Reserved.

Distributed in the United Kingdom by Macmillan Children's Books, a division of Pan Macmillan.

Library of Congress Cataloging-in-Publication Data

Kim, Derek Kirk.
 [Same difference and other stories.]
 Same difference / Derek Kirk Kim.
    p. cm.
 Summary: A series of short stories in graphic novel format follows a group
of friends in their twenties as they navigate young adulthood and
relationships.
 ISBN 978-1-59643-657-2
 1. Short stories, American. 2. Humorous stories. 3. Graphic novels. [1.
Graphic novels. 2. Interpersonal relations—Fiction. 3. Korean
Americans—Fiction. 4. Conduct of life—Fiction. 5. Short stories. 6.
Humorous stories.] I. Title.
 PZ7.7.K556Sam 2011
 741.5'973—dc22

                                        2010052663

First Second books are available for special promotions and premiums.
For details, contact: Director of Special Markets, Holtzbrinck Publishers.

FIRST

EDITION

Book design by Danica Novgorodoff and Derek Kirk Kim
Printed in China

10 9 8 7 6 5 4 3 2 1

Introduction

by Gene Yang

I first met Derek years ago in San Jose, California. I was patrolling the mean streets of downtown in hot pursuit of Dr. Demolisher when out of nowhere an electrified fist hit me square in the jaw. Invulnerability to electricity is one of my superpowers, but it still hurt like nobody's business. I looked up to see this Asian guy standing over me, with a cape flapping over his shoulder and a scowl under his domino mask. A teenager boy in brightly-colored spandex somersaulted over his shoulder. "Betta check yo'self before you wreck yo'self!" said the boy—his sidekick Brent, I later found out. Derek smirked as Brent poked a finger at my chest. It was on.

It took about an hour and a half of fisticuffs and witty banter for us to realize that we were all after Dr. Demolisher. Most of downtown lay in ruins by then, but, man, we had a laugh.

After that, we found a few other folks like us and formed a superteam. Those were probably the best days of my life. We built a secret base behind George Washington's eyeball on Mount Rushmore, and we parked our fleet of rocket ship and giant robots in his nose. We were on a real streak back then, putting superpowered perps behind bars on a monthly basis. People loved us for it. Twenty seven mayors gave us keys to their cities, twenty from our solar system and seven from the next one over.

It was during our battle with the cybernetic hordes from the Shadow Dimension—our android butler/historian refers to it as The Annihilation Initiative: Worlds Under Siege—that things started to fall apart. I began noticing a distant, glassy look in Derek's eye. He was still winning, of course—it's hard not to when you have the strength of 10,000 men—but even when his electrified fist was buried deep in the metal skull of a flesh-eating robot, you could tell his mind was somewhere else. I finally asked him about it. He crossed his arms and looked at his boots while Brent broke the news: Derek wanted to retire from our line of work, maybe try his hand at making funnybooks. My heart broke, but I did my best to hide it. This was my best friend, after all. Also, he was one of three sentient beings in the universe who knew that peanut brittle could neutralize all my powers.

"Why don't you do a memoir?" I suggested. Maybe drawing little doodles of his adventures would make him realize how silly it would be to give them up. "You've lived a pretty interesting life, and memoir graphic novels sell like hotcakes these days." Derek didn't look up.

"Nah," Brent said, mid-cartwheel. "He's gonna do something REALLY amazing."

SAME DIFFERENCE

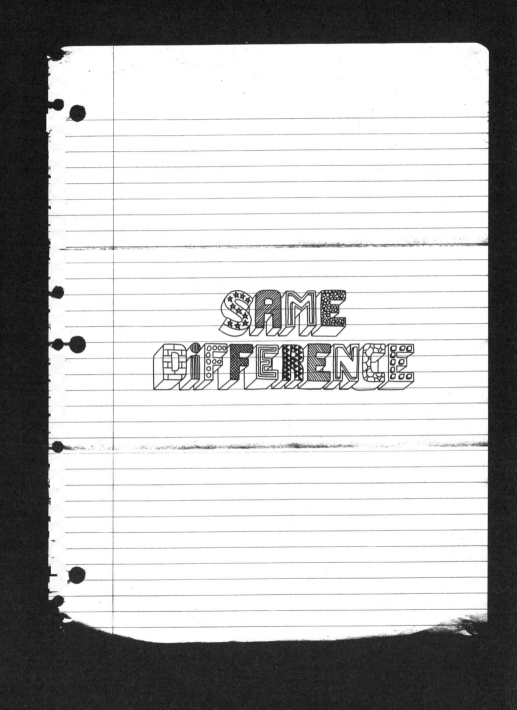

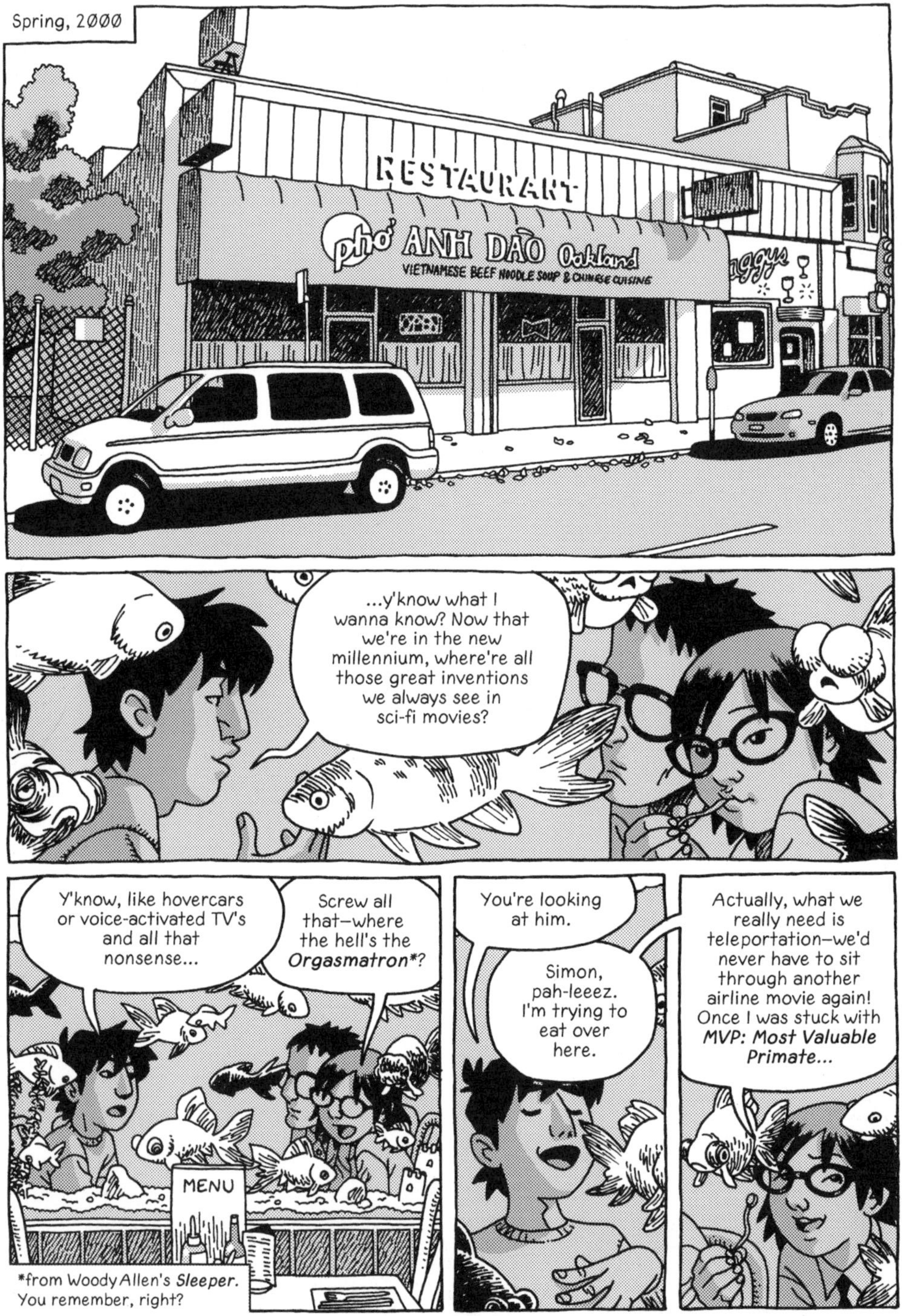
Spring, 2000
RESTAURANT
phở ANH DÀO Oakland
VIETNAMESE BEEF NOODLE SOUP & CHINESE CUISINE
...y'know what I wanna know? Now that we're in the new millennium, where're all those great inventions we always see in sci-fi movies?
Y'know, like hovercars or voice-activated TV's and all that nonsense...
Screw all that—where the hell's the ***Orgasmatron****?
MENU
*from Woody Allen's *Sleeper*. You remember, right?
You're looking at him.
Simon, pah-leeez. I'm trying to eat over here.
Actually, what we really need is teleportation—we'd never have to sit through another airline movie again! Once I was stuck with ***MVP: Most Valuable Primate...***

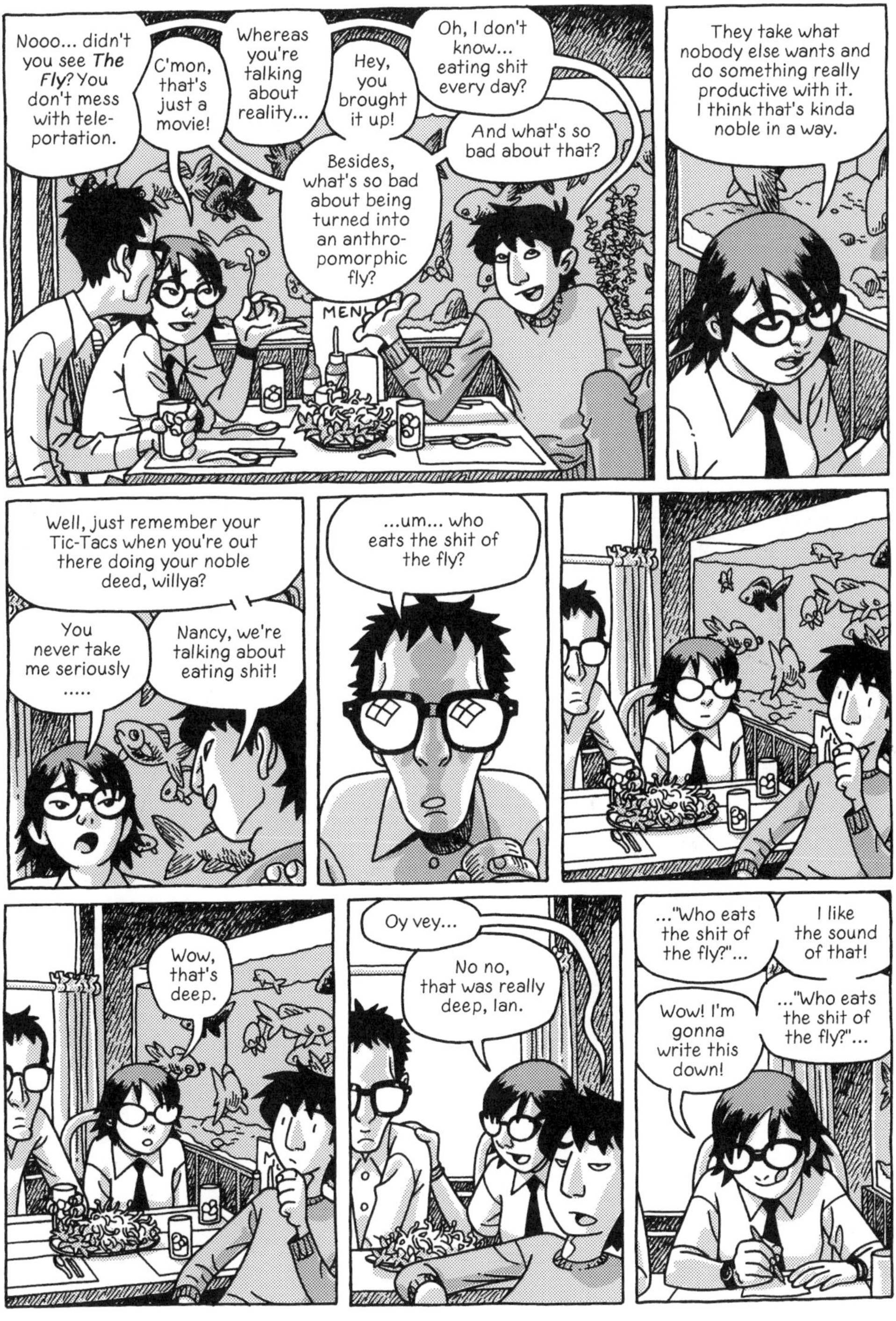
Nooo... didn't you see *The Fly*? You don't mess with tele-portation.
C'mon, that's just a movie!
Whereas you're talking about reality...
Hey, you brought it up!
Oh, I don't know... eating shit every day?
Besides, what's so bad about being turned into an anthro-pomorphic fly?
And what's so bad about that?
MENU
They take what nobody else wants and do something really productive with it. I think that's kinda noble in a way.
Well, just remember your Tic-Tacs when you're out there doing your noble deed, willya?
You never take me seriously .....
Nancy, we're talking about eating shit!
...um... who eats the shit of the fly?
Wow, that's deep.
Oy vey...
No no, that was really deep, Ian.
..."Who eats the shit of the fly?"...
I like the sound of that!
Wow! I'm gonna write this down!
..."Who eats the shit of the fly?"...

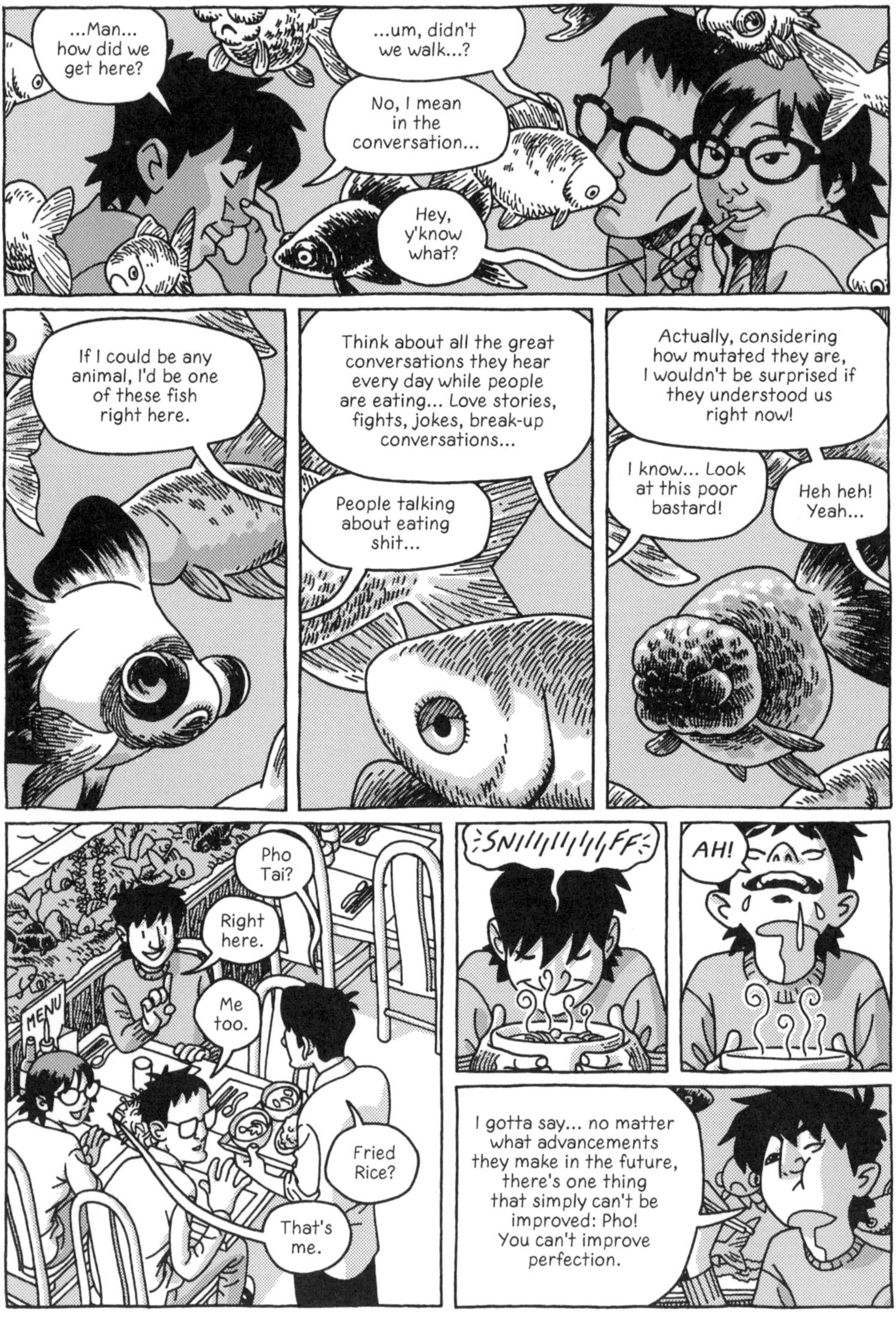
...Man... how did we get here?
...um, didn't we walk...?
No, I mean in the conversation...
Hey, y'know what?
If I could be any animal, I'd be one of these fish right here.
Think about all the great conversations they hear every day while people are eating... Love stories, fights, jokes, break-up conversations...
People talking about eating shit...
Actually, considering how mutated they are, I wouldn't be surprised if they understood us right now!
I know... Look at this poor bastard!
Heh heh! Yeah...
Pho Tai?
Right here.
Me too.
Fried Rice?
That's me.
MENU
SNIIIIIIIIFF
AH!
I gotta say... no matter what advancements they make in the future, there's one thing that simply can't be improved: Pho! You can't improve perfection.

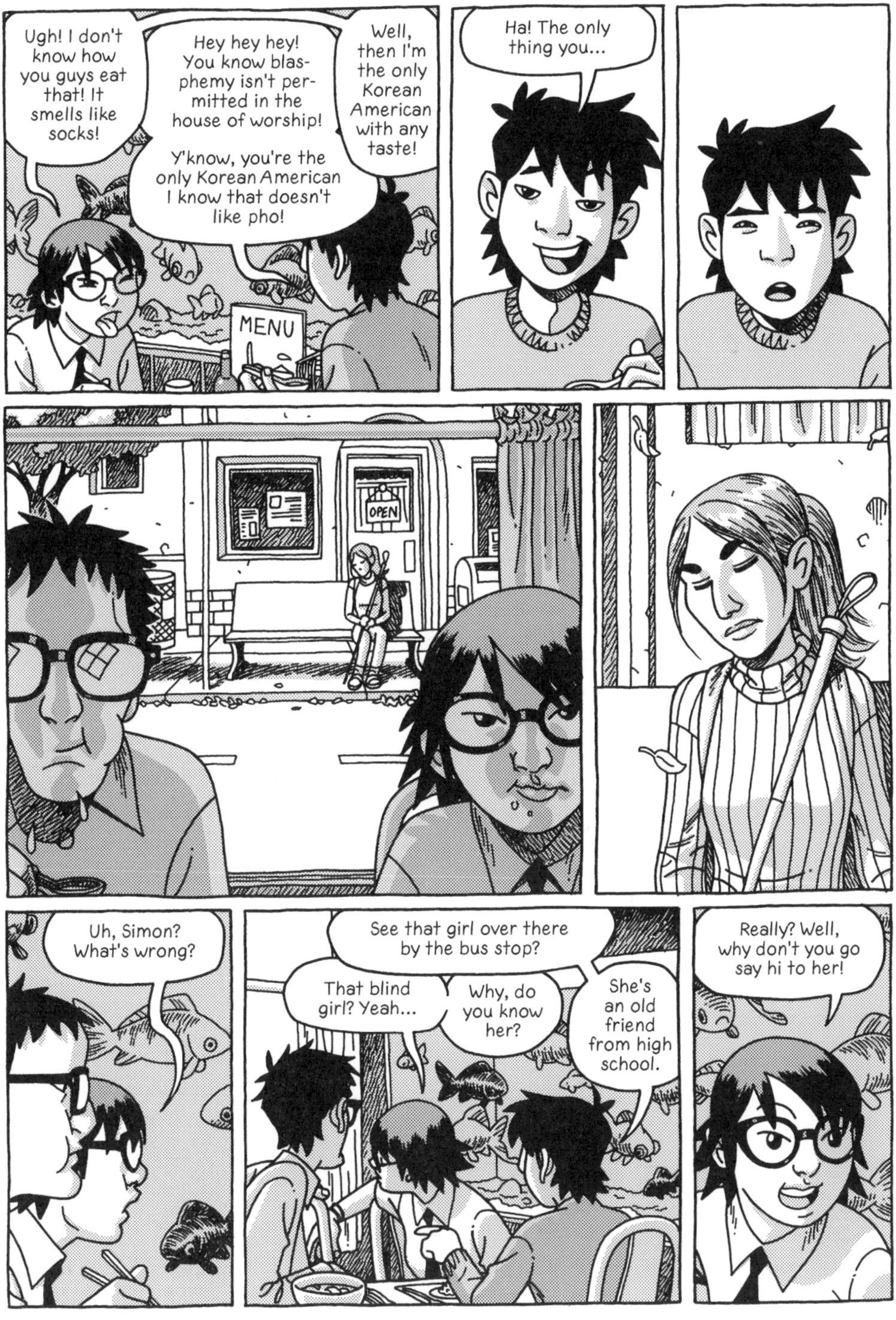
Ugh! I don't know how you guys eat that! It smells like socks!
Hey hey hey! You know blasphemy isn't permitted in the house of worship!
Y'know, you're the only Korean American I know that doesn't like pho!
Well, then I'm the only Korean American with any taste!
MENU
Ha! The only thing you...
OPEN
Uh, Simon? What's wrong?
See that girl over there by the bus stop?
That blind girl? Yeah...
Why, do you know her?
She's an old friend from high school.
Really? Well, why don't you go say hi to her!

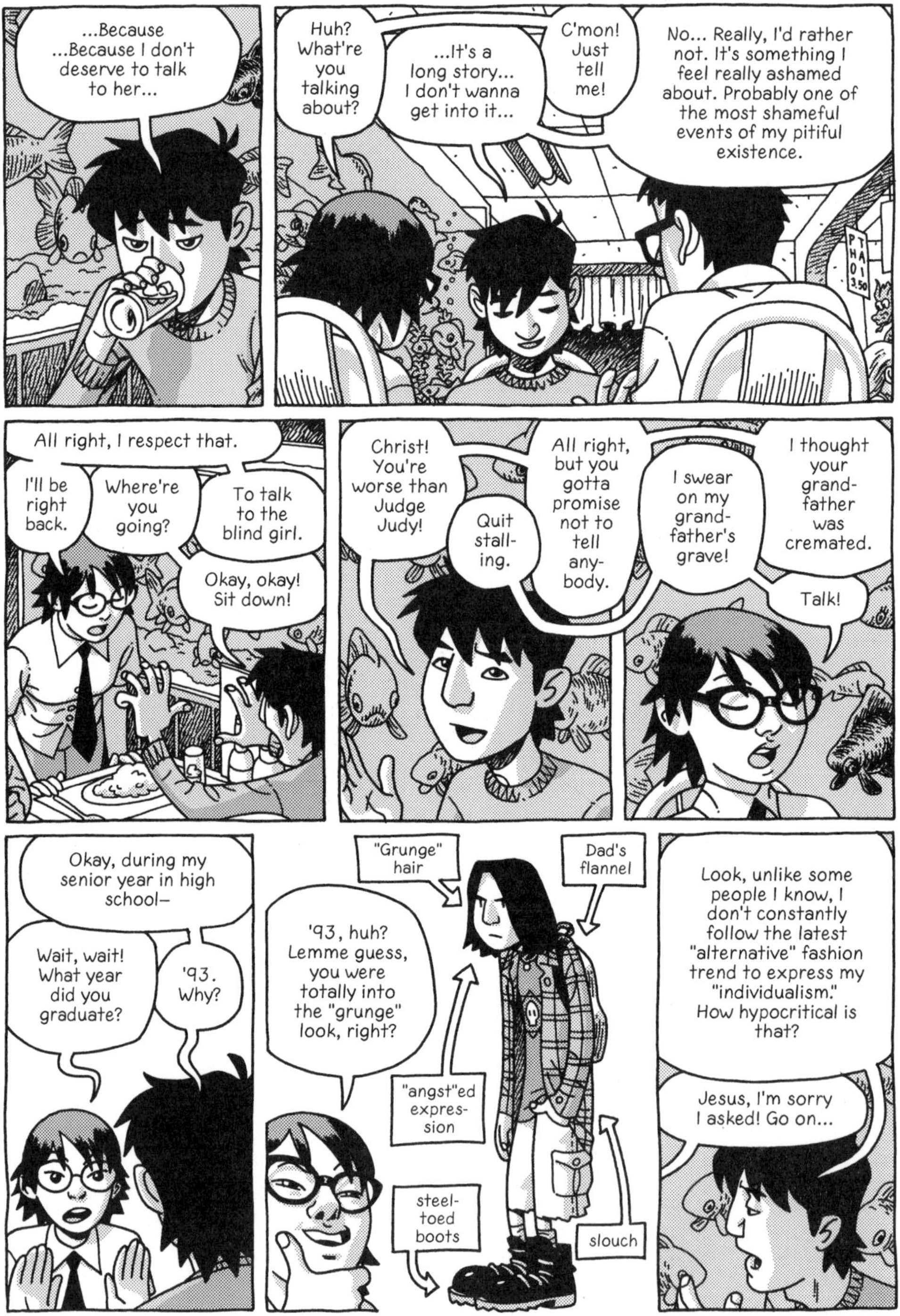
...Because
...Because I don't deserve to talk to her...
Huh? What're you talking about?
...It's a long story... I don't wanna get into it...
C'mon! Just tell me!
No... Really, I'd rather not. It's something I feel really ashamed about. Probably one of the most shameful events of my pitiful existence.
All right, I respect that.
I'll be right back.
Where're you going?
To talk to the blind girl.
Okay, okay! Sit down!
Christ! You're worse than Judge Judy!
Quit stalling.
All right, but you gotta promise not to tell anybody.
I swear on my grandfather's grave!
I thought your grandfather was cremated.
Talk!
Okay, during my senior year in high school–
Wait, wait! What year did you graduate?
'93. Why?
'93, huh? Lemme guess, you were totally into the "grunge" look, right?
"Grunge" hair
Dad's flannel
"angst"ed expression
steel-toed boots
slouch
Look, unlike some people I know, I don't constantly follow the latest "alternative" fashion trend to express my "individualism." How hypocritical is that?
Jesus, I'm sorry I asked! Go on...

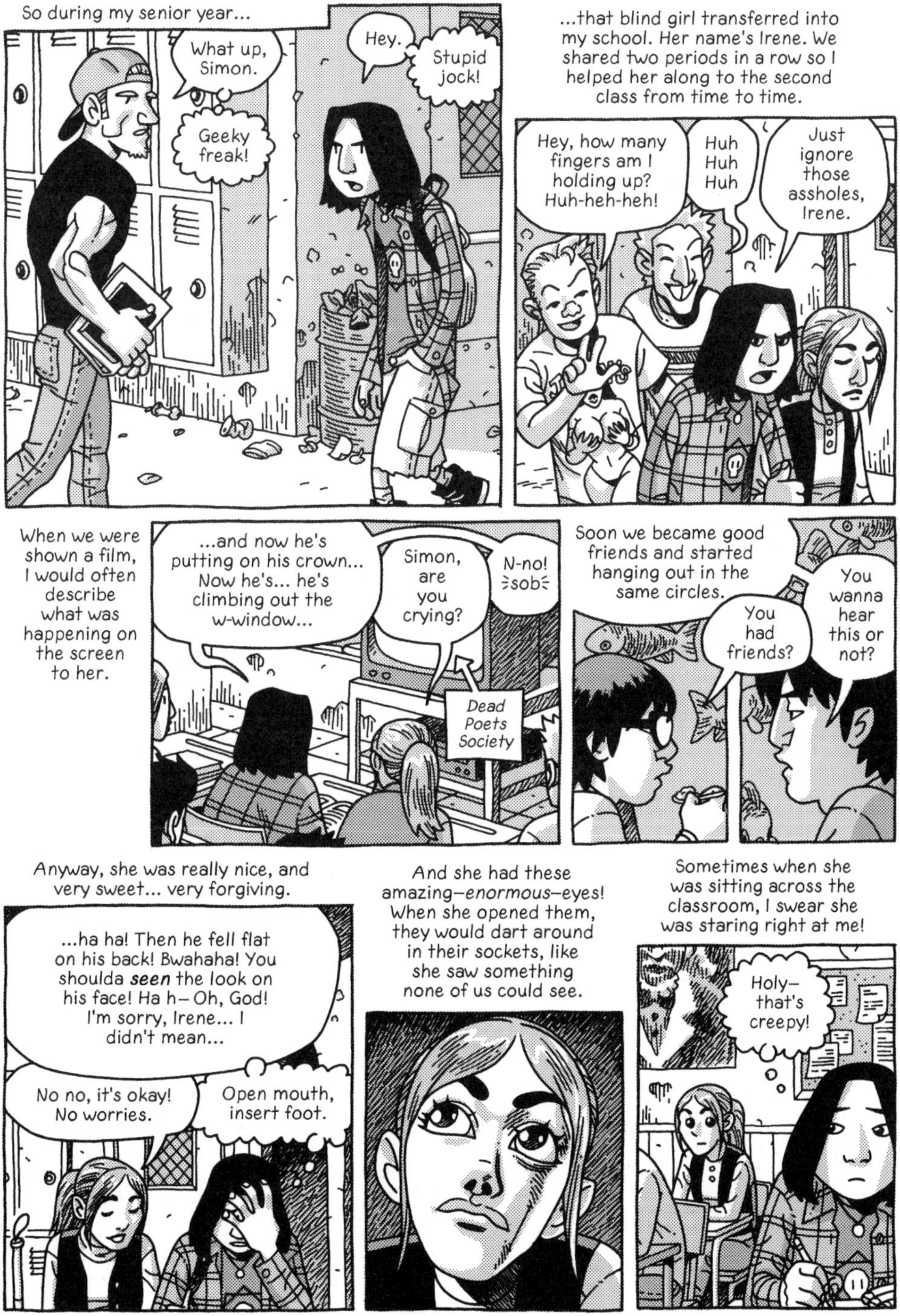
So during my senior year...
What up, Simon.
Geeky freak!
Hey.
Stupid jock!
...that blind girl transferred into my school. Her name's Irene. We shared two periods in a row so I helped her along to the second class from time to time.
Hey, how many fingers am I holding up? Huh-heh-heh!
Huh Huh Huh
Just ignore those assholes, Irene.
When we were shown a film, I would often describe what was happening on the screen to her.
...and now he's putting on his crown... Now he's... he's climbing out the w-window...
Simon, are you crying?
N-no! sob
Dead Poets Society
Soon we became good friends and started hanging out in the same circles.
You had friends?
You wanna hear this or not?
Anyway, she was really nice, and very sweet... very forgiving.
...ha ha! Then he fell flat on his back! Bwahaha! You shoulda seen the look on his face! Ha h– Oh, God! I'm sorry, Irene... I didn't mean...
No no, it's okay! No worries.
Open mouth, insert foot.
And she had these amazing–enormous–eyes! When she opened them, they would dart around in their sockets, like she saw something none of us could see.
Sometimes when she was sitting across the classroom, I swear she was staring right at me!
Holy– that's creepy!

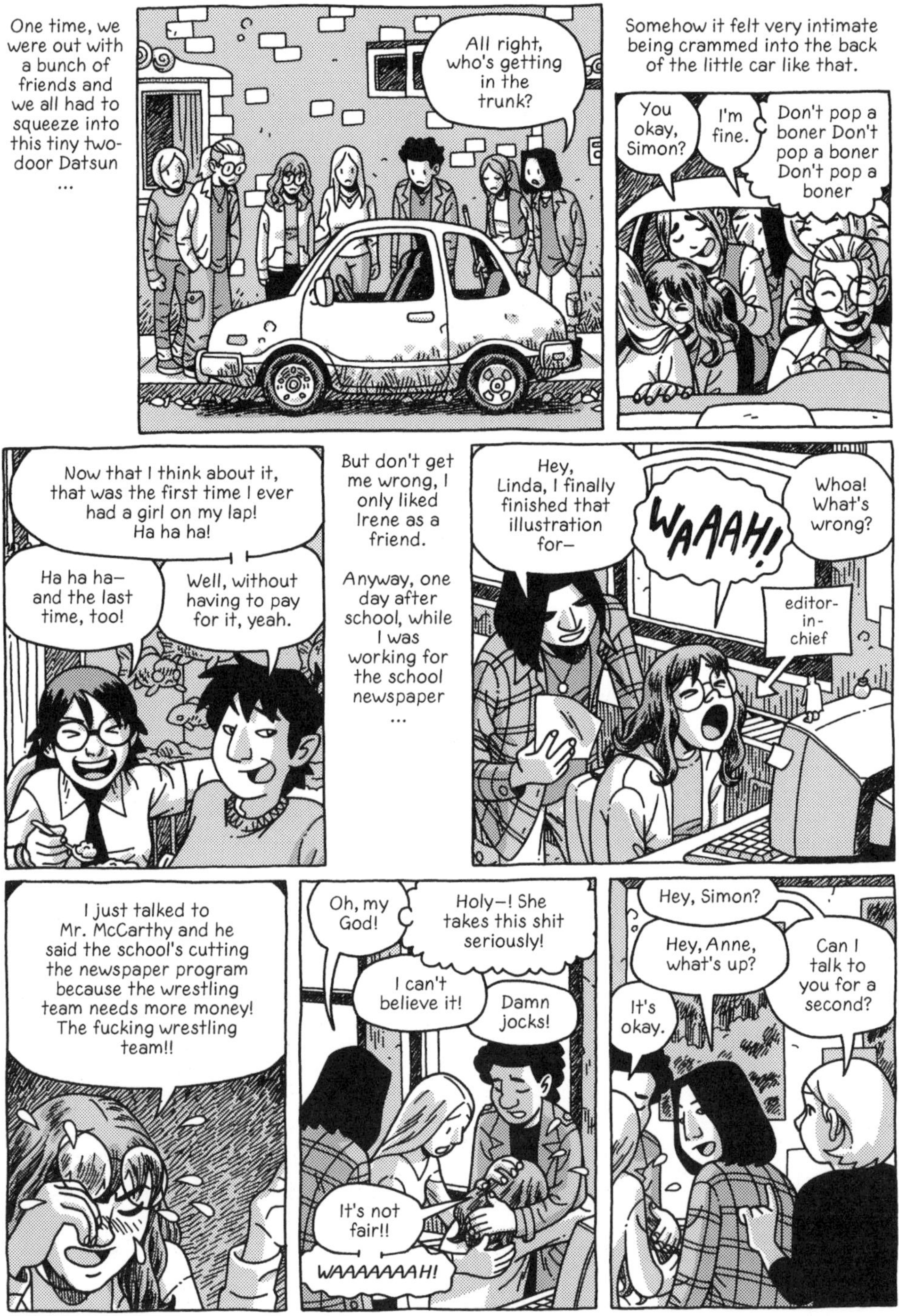
One time, we were out with a bunch of friends and we all had to squeeze into this tiny two-door Datsun …
All right, who's getting in the trunk?
Somehow it felt very intimate being crammed into the back of the little car like that.
You okay, Simon?
I'm fine.
Don't pop a boner Don't pop a boner Don't pop a boner
Now that I think about it, that was the first time I ever had a girl on my lap! Ha ha ha!
Ha ha ha— and the last time, too!
Well, without having to pay for it, yeah.
But don't get me wrong, I only liked Irene as a friend.
Anyway, one day after school, while I was working for the school newspaper …
Hey, Linda, I finally finished that illustration for—
WAAAH!
Whoa! What's wrong?
editor-in-chief
I just talked to Mr. McCarthy and he said the school's cutting the newspaper program because the wrestling team needs more money! The fucking wrestling team!!
Oh, my God!
Holy—! She takes this shit seriously!
I can't believe it!
Damn jocks!
It's not fair!!
WAAAAAAAH!
Hey, Simon?
Hey, Anne, what's up?
It's okay.
Can I talk to you for a second?

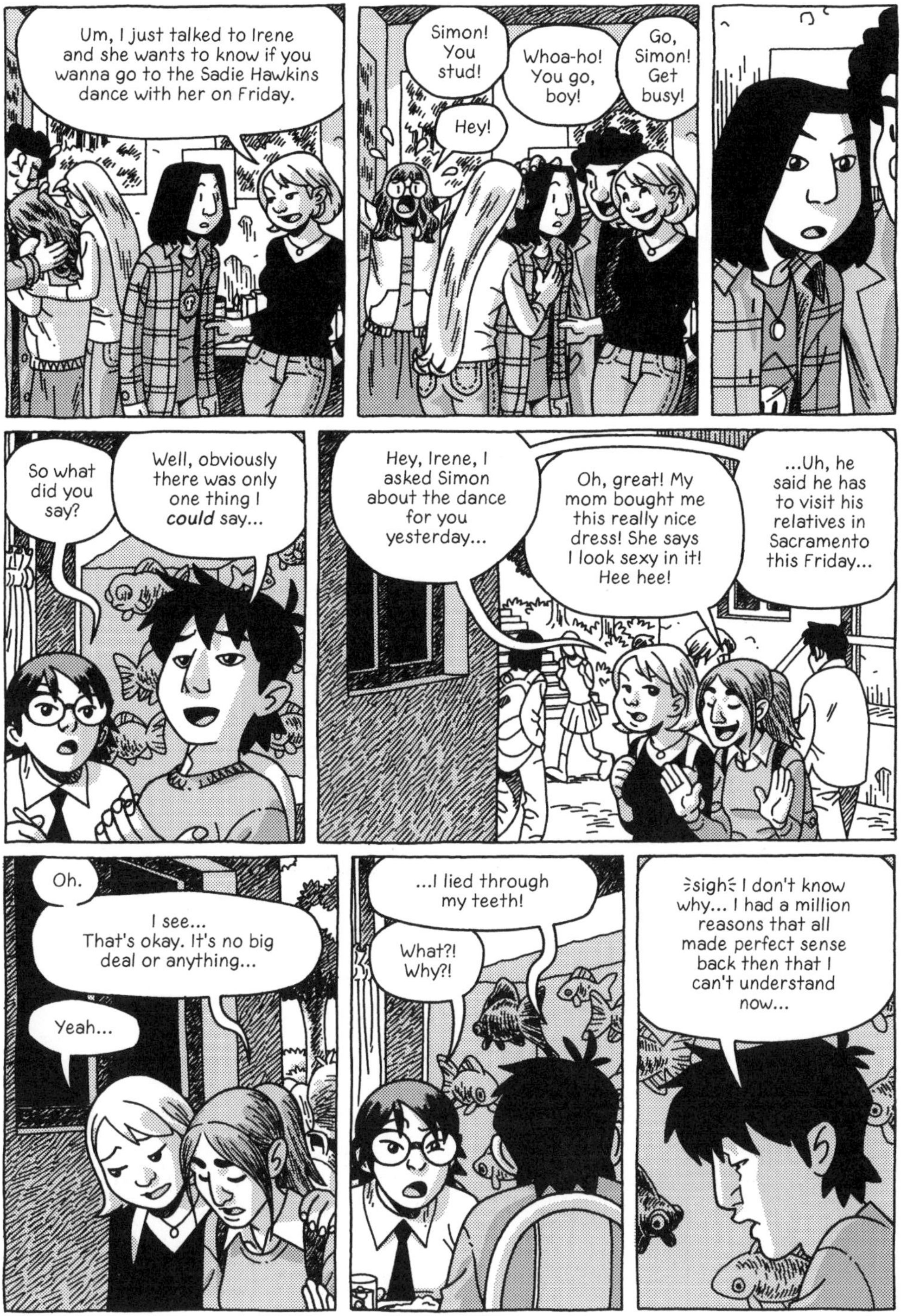

Um, I just talked to Irene and she wants to know if you wanna go to the Sadie Hawkins dance with her on Friday.
Simon! You stud!
Hey!
Whoa-ho! You go, boy!
Go, Simon! Get busy!
So what did you say?
Well, obviously there was only one thing I *could* say...
Hey, Irene, I asked Simon about the dance for you yesterday...
Oh, great! My mom bought me this really nice dress! She says I look sexy in it! Hee hee!
...Uh, he said he has to visit his relatives in Sacramento this Friday...
Oh.
I see... That's okay. It's no big deal or anything...
Yeah...
...I lied through my teeth!
What?! Why?!
⁼sigh⁼ I don't know why... I had a million reasons that all made perfect sense back then that I can't understand now...

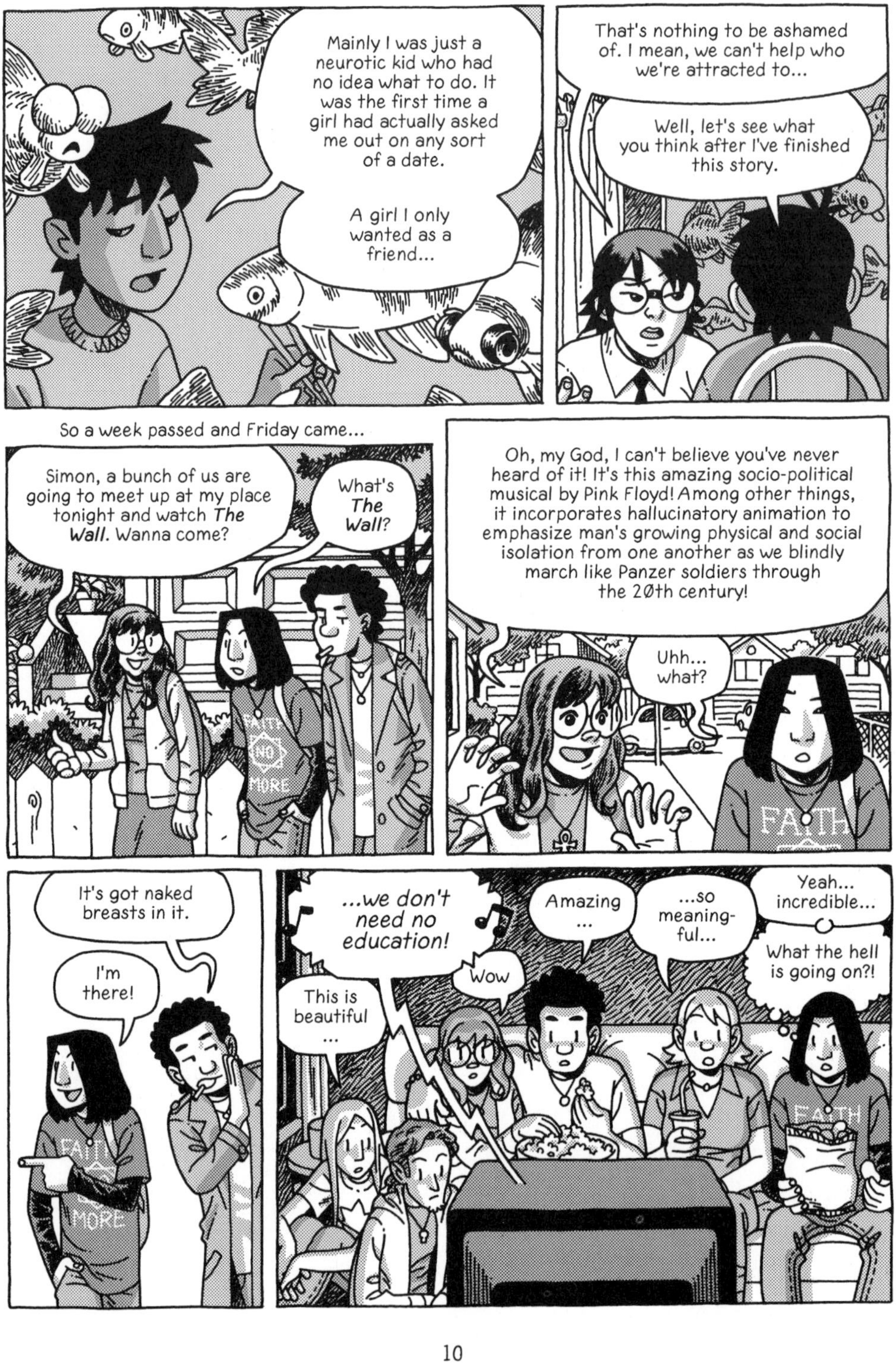
Mainly I was just a neurotic kid who had no idea what to do. It was the first time a girl had actually asked me out on any sort of a date.
A girl I only wanted as a friend...
That's nothing to be ashamed of. I mean, we can't help who we're attracted to...
Well, let's see what you think after I've finished this story.
So a week passed and Friday came...
Simon, a bunch of us are going to meet up at my place tonight and watch *The Wall*. Wanna come?
What's *The Wall*?
Oh, my God, I can't believe you've never heard of it! It's this amazing socio-political musical by Pink Floyd! Among other things, it incorporates hallucinatory animation to emphasize man's growing physical and social isolation from one another as we blindly march like Panzer soldiers through the 20th century!
Uhh... what?
It's got naked breasts in it.
I'm there!
...we don't need no education!
This is beautiful ...
Wow
Amazing ...
...so meaning-ful...
Yeah... incredible...
What the hell is going on?!

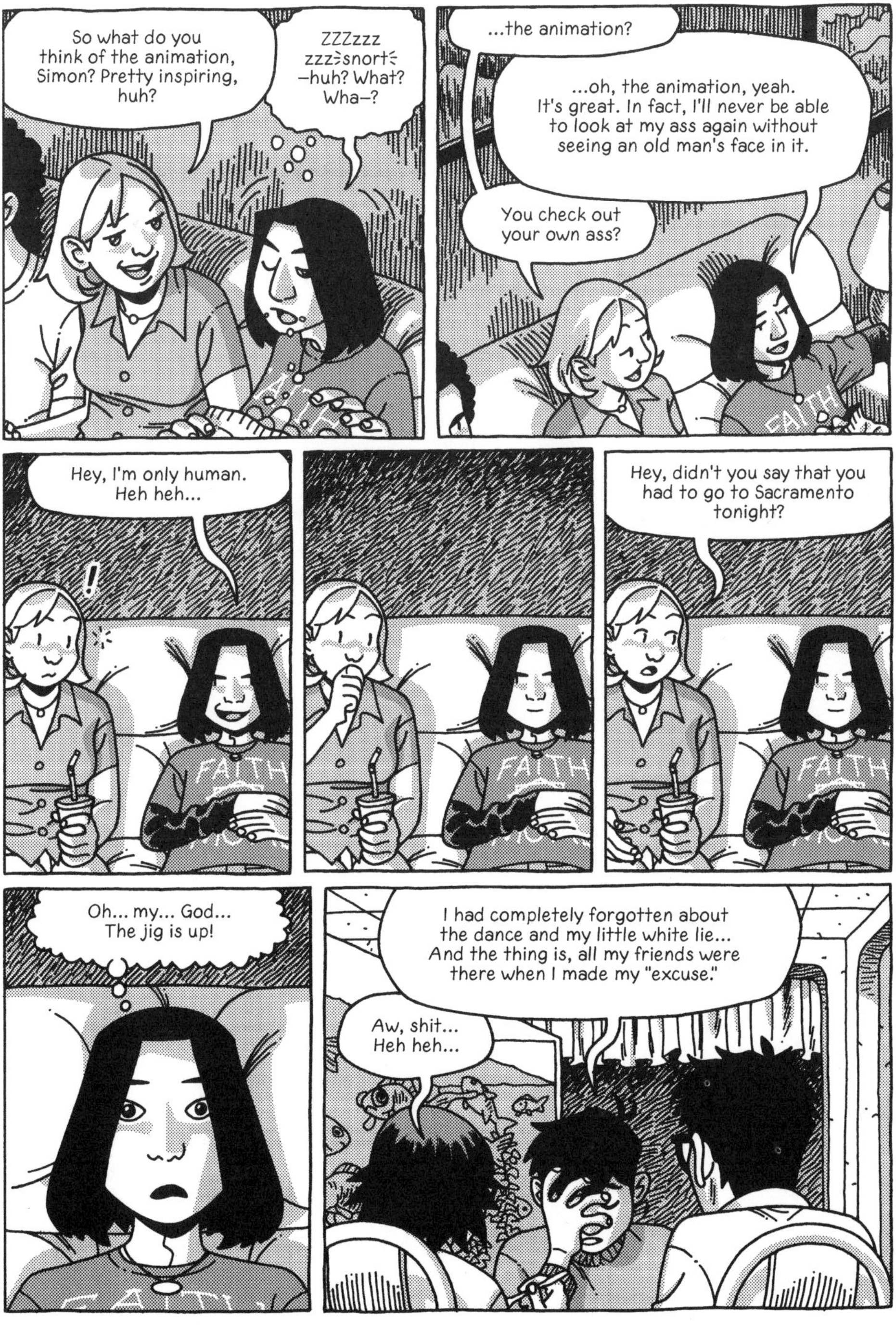

So what do you think of the animation, Simon? Pretty inspiring, huh?
ZZZzzz zzz≥snort≤ –huh? What? Wha–?
...the animation?
...oh, the animation, yeah. It's great. In fact, I'll never be able to look at my ass again without seeing an old man's face in it.
You check out your own ass?
Hey, I'm only human. Heh heh...
!
Hey, didn't you say that you had to go to Sacramento tonight?
Oh... my... God... The jig is up!
I had completely forgotten about the dance and my little white lie... And the thing is, all my friends were there when I made my "excuse."
Aw, shit... Heh heh...

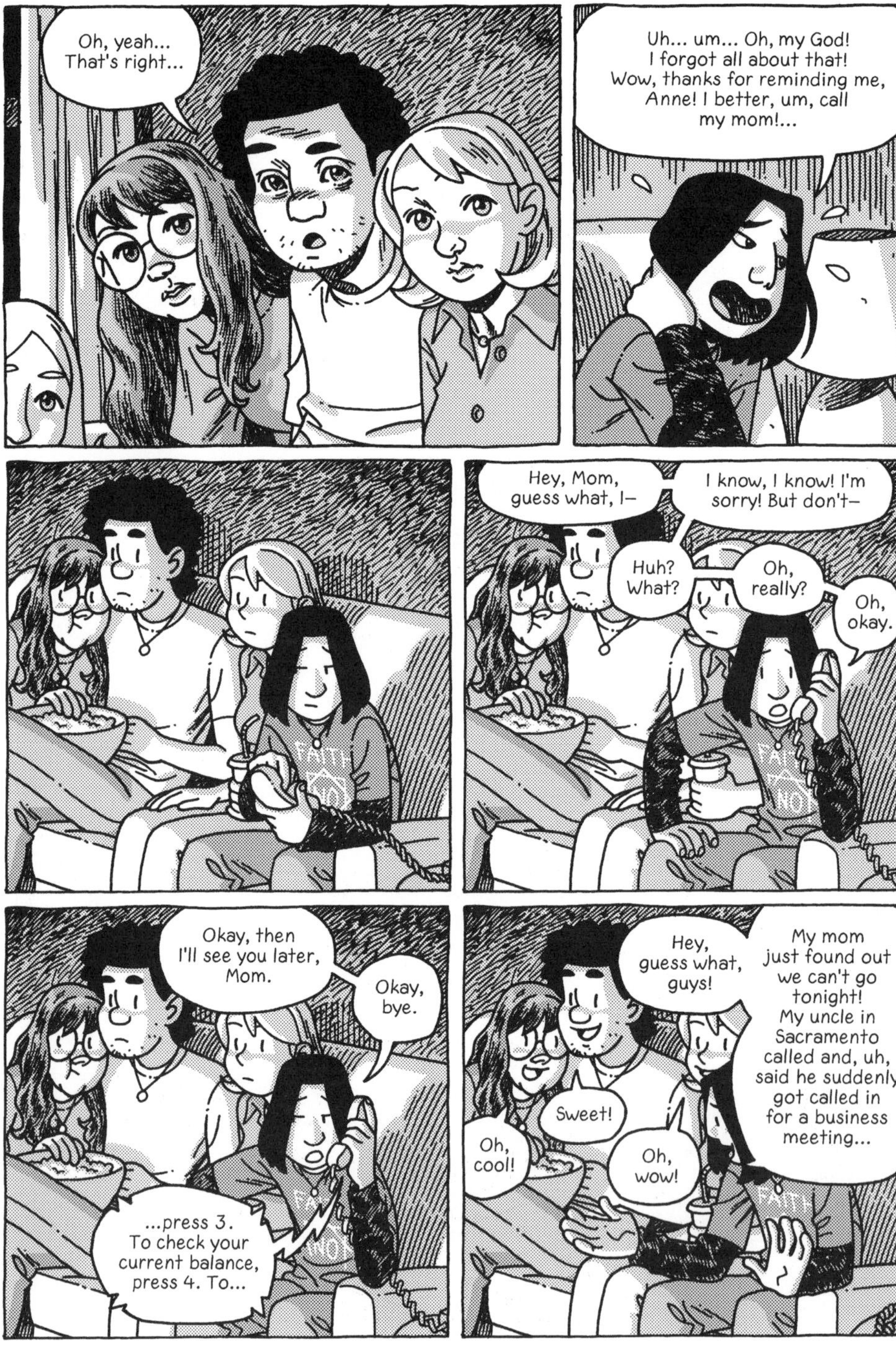
Oh, yeah... That's right...
Uh... um... Oh, my God! I forgot all about that! Wow, thanks for reminding me, Anne! I better, um, call my mom!...
Hey, Mom, guess what, I—
I know, I know! I'm sorry! But don't—
Huh? What?
Oh, really?
Oh, okay.
Okay, then I'll see you later, Mom.
Okay, bye.
...press 3. To check your current balance, press 4. To...
Hey, guess what, guys!
My mom just found out we can't go tonight! My uncle in Sacramento called and, uh, said he suddenly got called in for a business meeting...
Sweet!
Oh, cool!
Oh, wow!

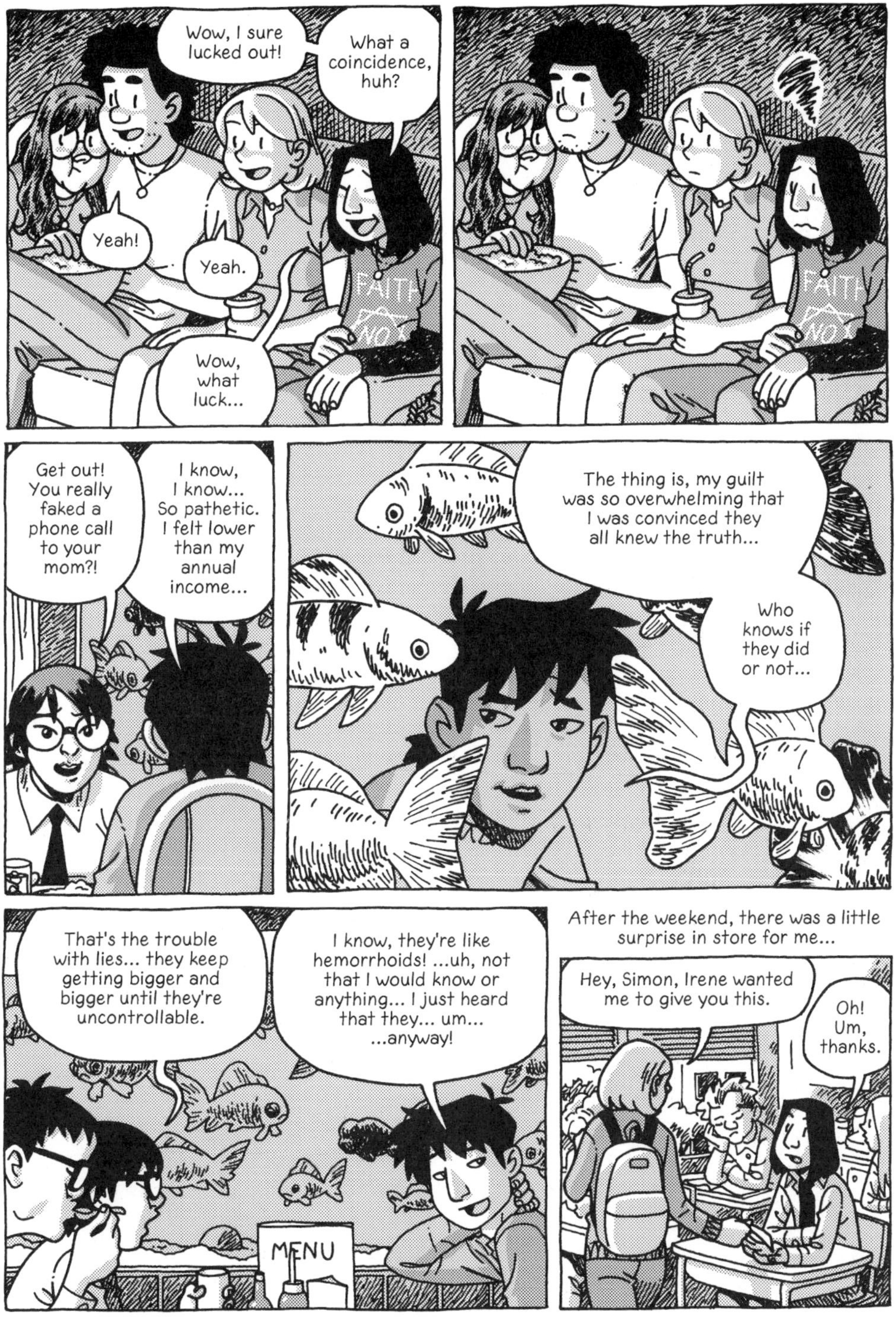
Wow, I sure lucked out!
What a coincidence, huh?
Yeah!
Yeah.
Wow, what luck...
FAITH NO
FAITH NO
Get out! You really faked a phone call to your mom?!
I know, I know... So pathetic. I felt lower than my annual income...
The thing is, my guilt was so overwhelming that I was convinced they all knew the truth...
Who knows if they did or not...
That's the trouble with lies... they keep getting bigger and bigger until they're uncontrollable.
I know, they're like hemorrhoids! ...uh, not that I would know or anything... I just heard that they... um... ...anyway!
MENU
After the weekend, there was a little surprise in store for me...
Hey, Simon, Irene wanted me to give you this.
Oh! Um, thanks.

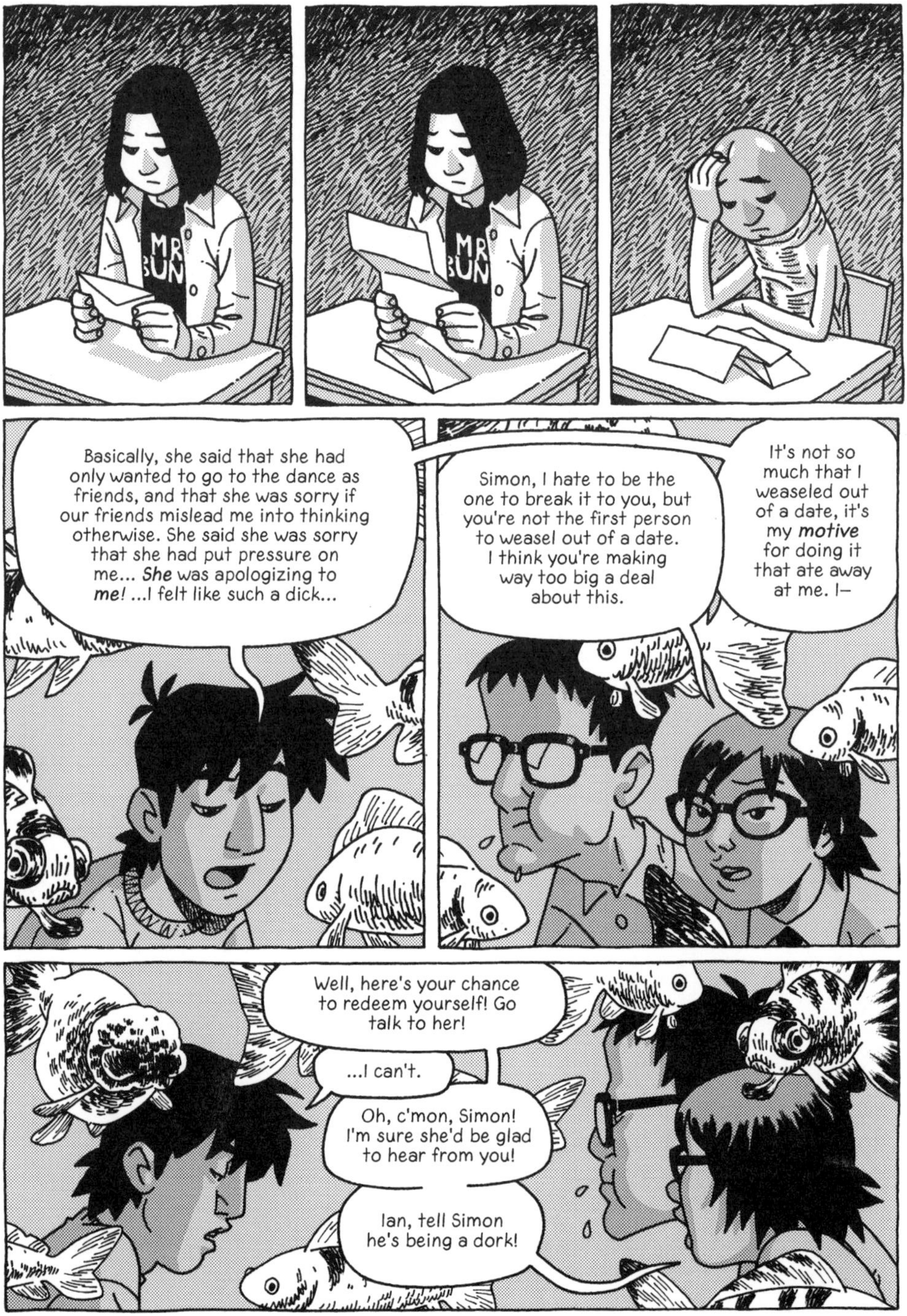
MR BUN
Basically, she said that she had only wanted to go to the dance as friends, and that she was sorry if our friends mislead me into thinking otherwise. She said she was sorry that she had put pressure on me... *She* was apologizing to *me!* ...I felt like such a dick...
Simon, I hate to be the one to break it to you, but you're not the first person to weasel out of a date. I think you're making way too big a deal about this.
It's not so much that I weaseled out of a date, it's my *motive* for doing it that ate away at me. I–
Well, here's your chance to redeem yourself! Go talk to her!
...I can't.
Oh, c'mon, Simon! I'm sure she'd be glad to hear from you!
Ian, tell Simon he's being a dork!

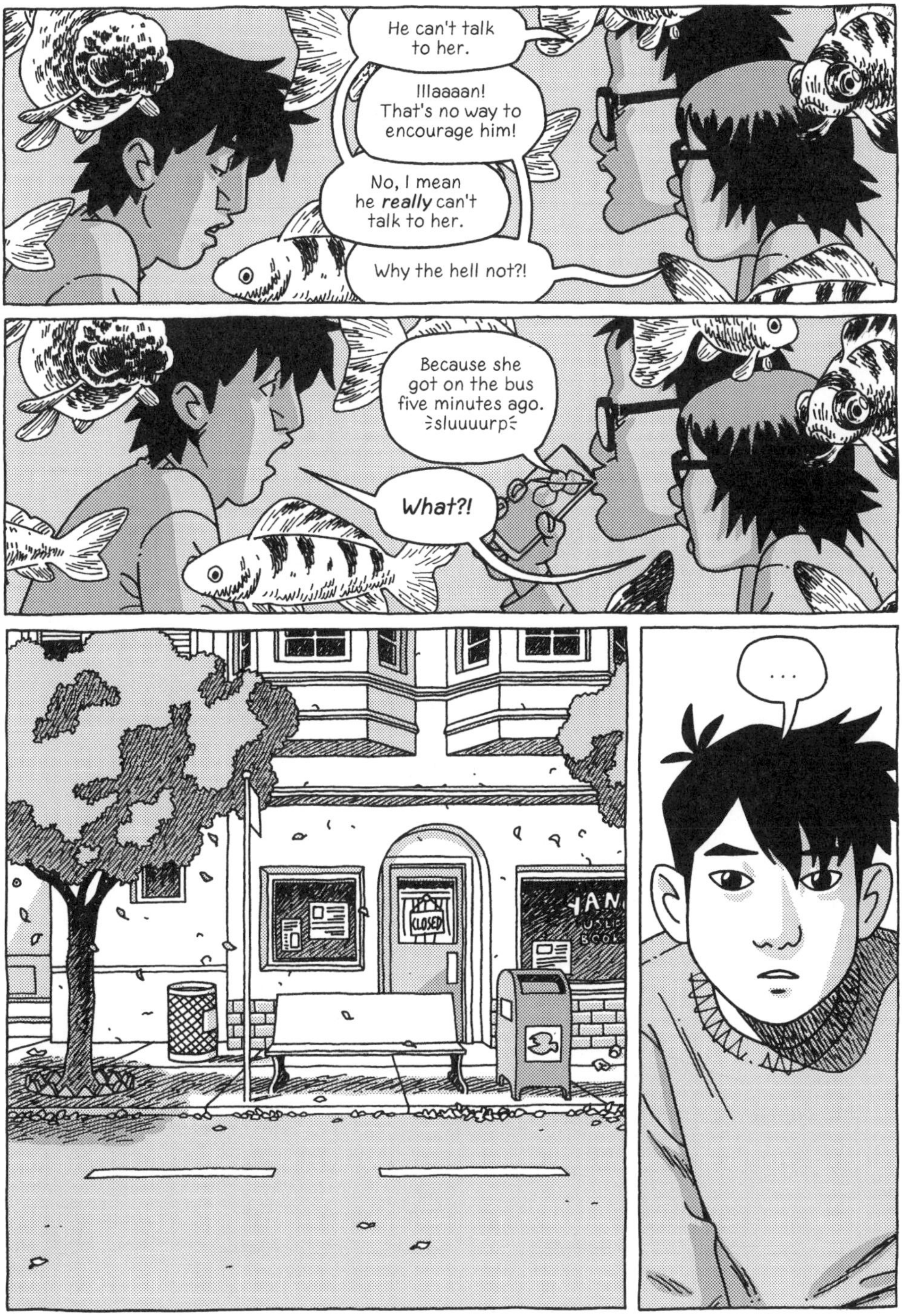
He can't talk to her.
IIlaaaan! That's no way to encourage him!
No, I mean he *really* can't talk to her.
Why the hell not?!
Because she got on the bus five minutes ago.
sluuuurp
What?!
CLOSED
...

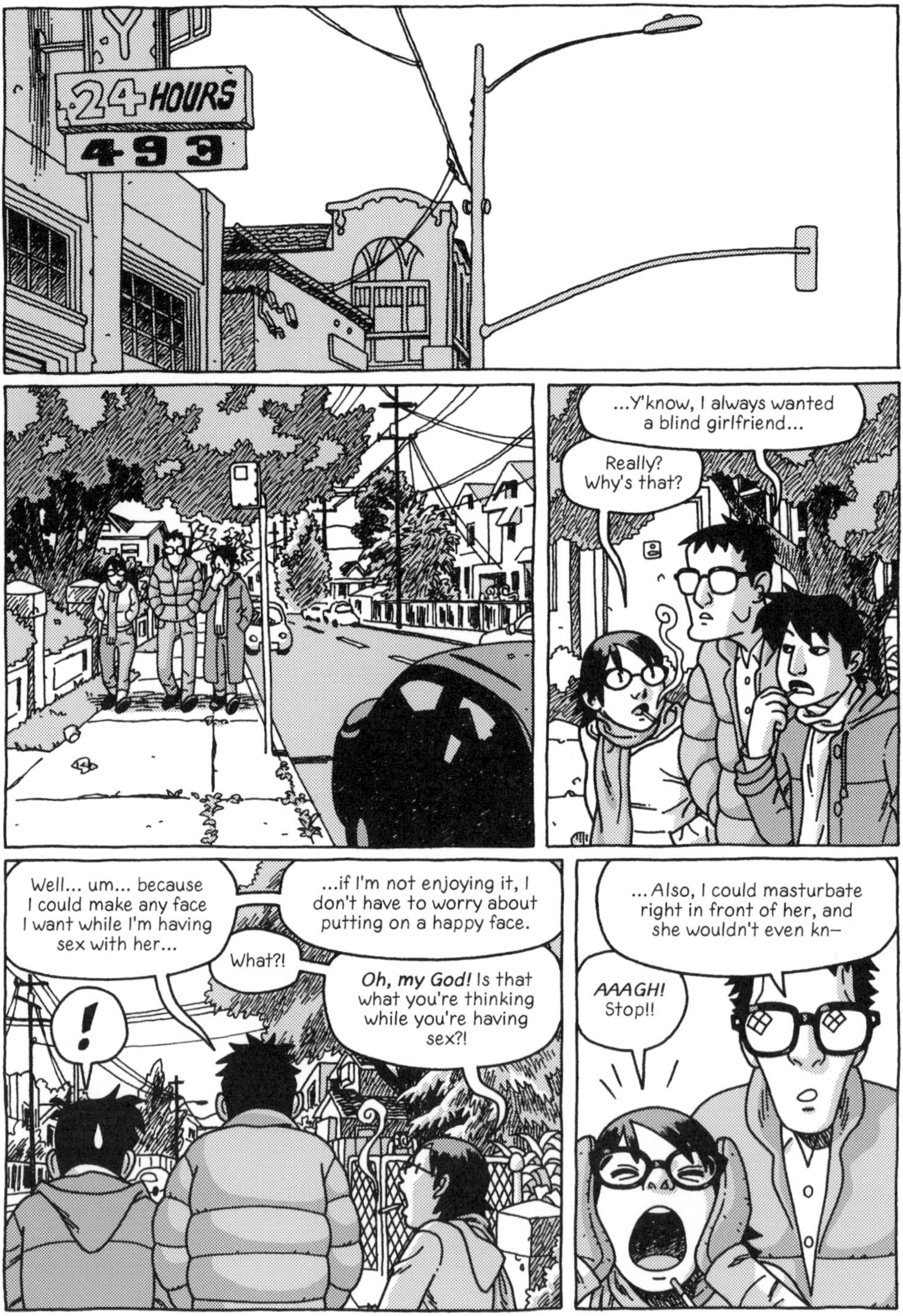
24 HOURS
493
...Y'know, I always wanted a blind girlfriend...
Really? Why's that?
Well... um... because I could make any face I want while I'm having sex with her...
!
What?!
...if I'm not enjoying it, I don't have to worry about putting on a happy face.
Oh, my God! Is that what you're thinking while you're having sex?!
...Also, I could masturbate right in front of her, and she wouldn't even kn–
AAAGH! Stop!!

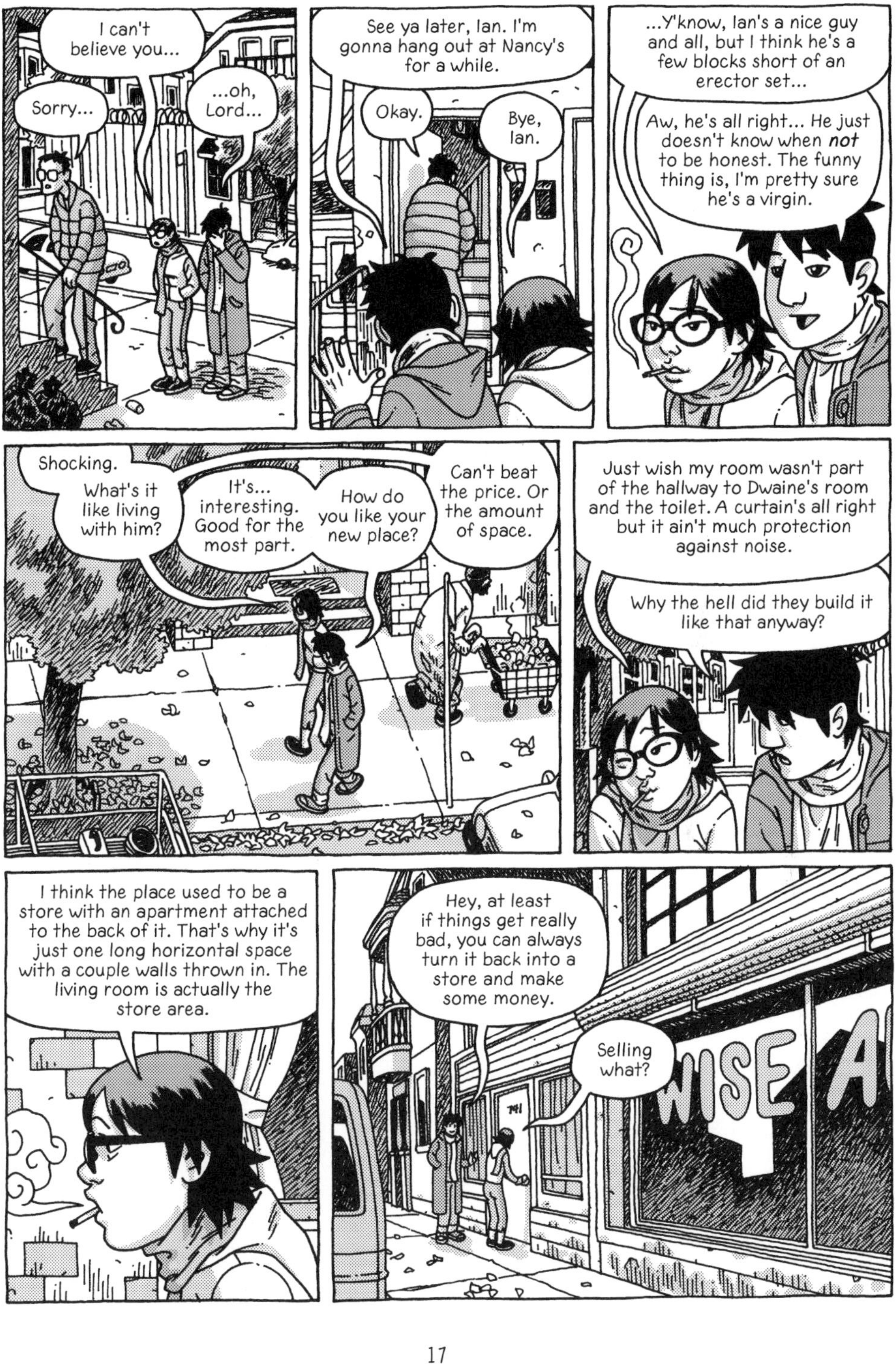
I can't believe you...
Sorry...
...oh, Lord...
See ya later, Ian. I'm gonna hang out at Nancy's for a while.
Okay.
Bye, Ian.
...Y'know, Ian's a nice guy and all, but I think he's a few blocks short of an erector set...
Aw, he's all right... He just doesn't know when ***not*** to be honest. The funny thing is, I'm pretty sure he's a virgin.
Shocking.
What's it like living with him?
It's... interesting. Good for the most part.
How do you like your new place?
Can't beat the price. Or the amount of space.
Just wish my room wasn't part of the hallway to Dwaine's room and the toilet. A curtain's all right but it ain't much protection against noise.
Why the hell did they build it like that anyway?
I think the place used to be a store with an apartment attached to the back of it. That's why it's just one long horizontal space with a couple walls thrown in. The living room is actually the store area.
Hey, at least if things get really bad, you can always turn it back into a store and make some money.
Selling what?
WISE A

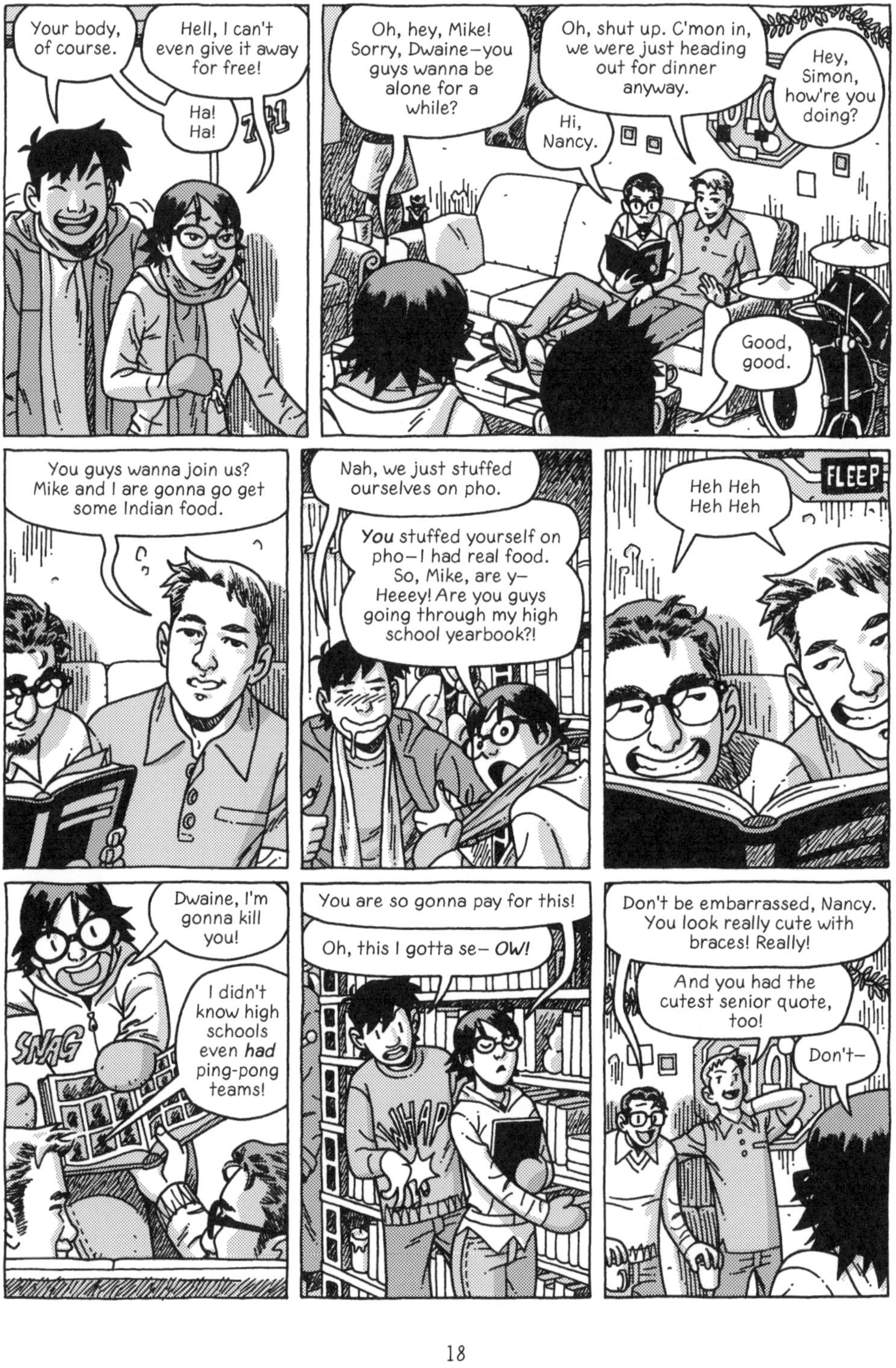
Your body, of course.
Hell, I can't even give it away for free!
Ha! Ha!
Oh, hey, Mike! Sorry, Dwaine—you guys wanna be alone for a while?
Oh, shut up. C'mon in, we were just heading out for dinner anyway.
Hi, Nancy.
Hey, Simon, how're you doing?
Good, good.
You guys wanna join us? Mike and I are gonna go get some Indian food.
Nah, we just stuffed ourselves on pho.
You stuffed yourself on pho—I had real food. So, Mike, are y— Heeey! Are you guys going through my high school yearbook?!
Heh Heh Heh Heh
FLEEP
Dwaine, I'm gonna kill you!
SNAG
I didn't know high schools even *had* ping-pong teams!
You are so gonna pay for this!
Oh, this I gotta se— *OW!*
WHAP
Don't be embarrassed, Nancy. You look really cute with braces! Really!
And you had the cutest senior quote, too!
Don't—

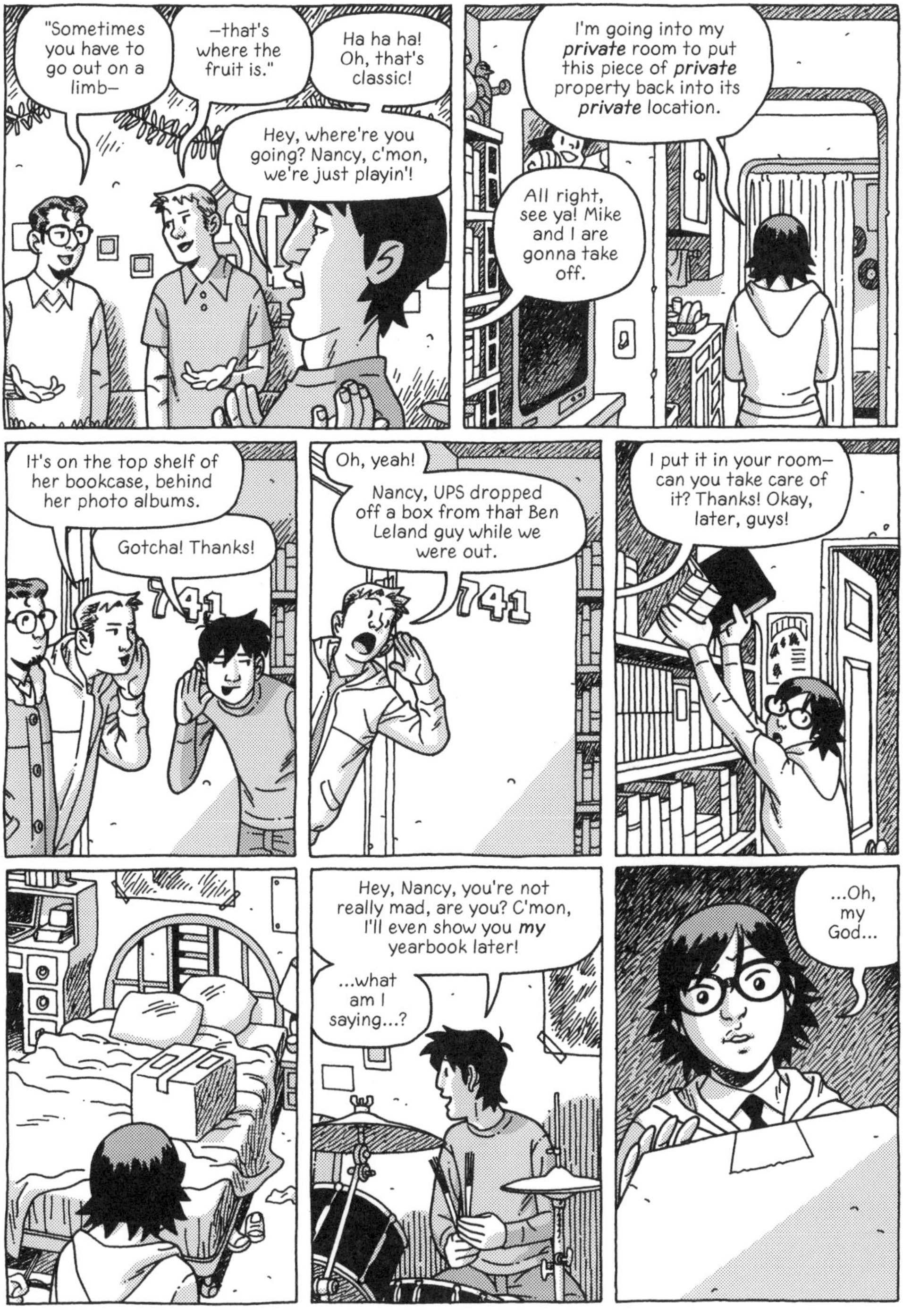
"Sometimes you have to go out on a limb–
–that's where the fruit is."
Ha ha ha! Oh, that's classic!
Hey, where're you going? Nancy, c'mon, we're just playin'!
I'm going into my *private* room to put this piece of *private* property back into its *private* location.
All right, see ya! Mike and I are gonna take off.
It's on the top shelf of her bookcase, behind her photo albums.
Gotcha! Thanks!
741
Oh, yeah!
Nancy, UPS dropped off a box from that Ben Leland guy while we were out.
741
I put it in your room– can you take care of it? Thanks! Okay, later, guys!
Hey, Nancy, you're not really mad, are you? C'mon, I'll even show you *my* yearbook later!
...what am I saying...?
...Oh, my God...

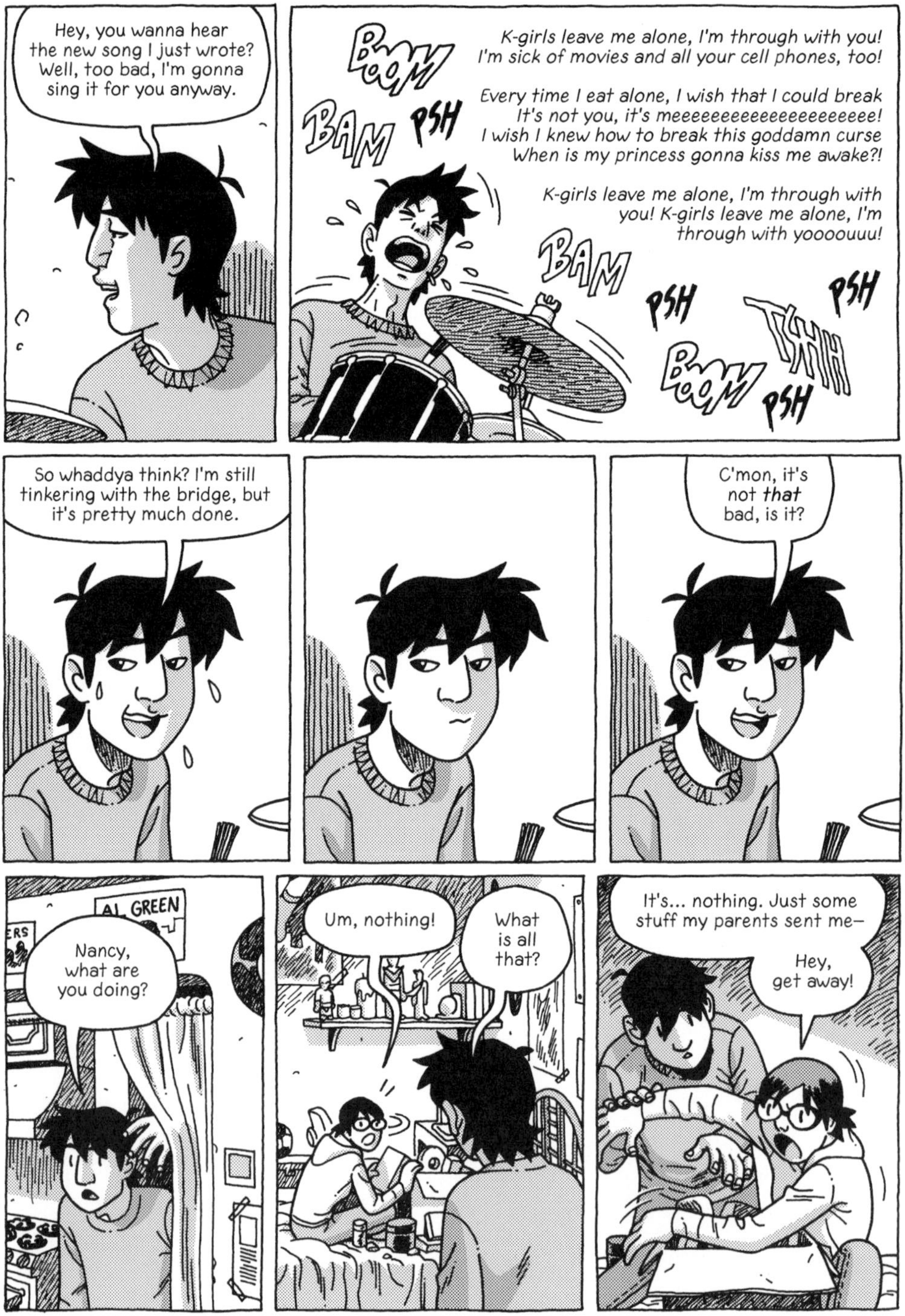
Hey, you wanna hear the new song I just wrote? Well, too bad, I'm gonna sing it for you anyway.
BOOOM
BAM
PSH
K-girls leave me alone, I'm through with you! I'm sick of movies and all your cell phones, too!
Every time I eat alone, I wish that I could break It's not you, it's meeeeeeeeeeeeeeeeeeeee! I wish I knew how to break this goddamn curse When is my princess gonna kiss me awake?!
K-girls leave me alone, I'm through with you! K-girls leave me alone, I'm through with yoooouuu!
BAM
PSH
TSHH
PSH
BOOOM
PSH
So whaddya think? I'm still tinkering with the bridge, but it's pretty much done.
C'mon, it's not *that* bad, is it?
AL GREEN
ERS
Nancy, what are you doing?
Um, nothing!
What is all that?
It's... nothing. Just some stuff my parents sent me—
Hey, get away!

What are you being so secretive for? Your parents sent you a shrunken head or something?

Simon—!

What the...?

...oh! I might as well just tell you!

But this doesn't leave the room, y'hear me?

Oh, God. I don't think I wanna know anymore...

Ever since Dwaine and I moved in here a couple months ago, we've been getting a letter **every** week from this guy named "Ben Leland".

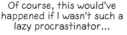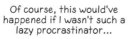

...again?!

It's always addressed to "Sarah Richardson," who must've been the tenant before us. I kept saving them up, meaning to send them back to him...

...No, no, I'll do it, don't worry. I just didn't get a chance to go outside today cause of the Robotech marathon on PBS...

Of course, this would've happened if I wasn't such a lazy procrastinator...

One day after class, I was really bored...

...and curiosity got the best of me...

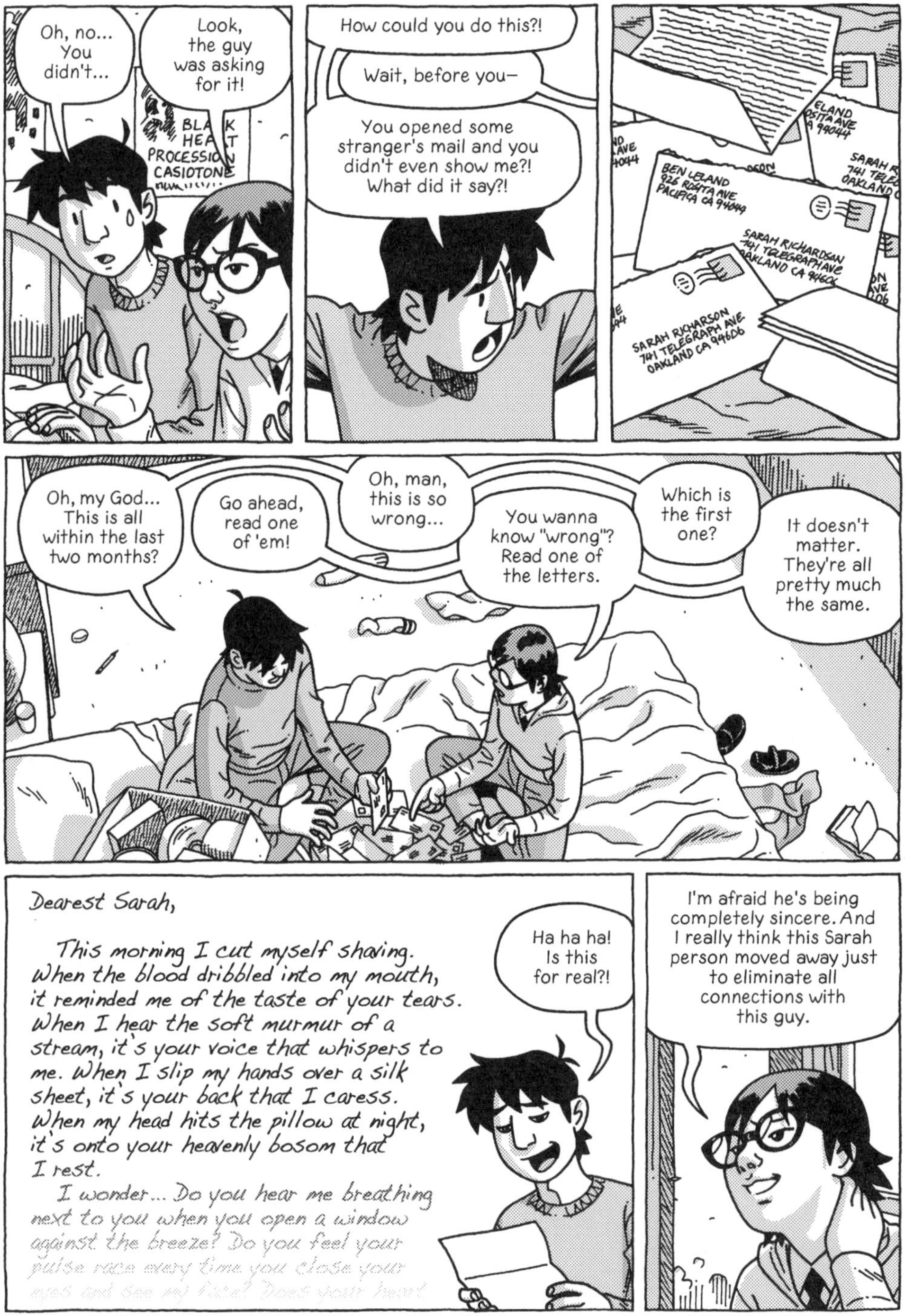
Oh, no... You didn't...
Look, the guy was asking for it!
BLACK HEART PROCESSION
CASIOTONE
How could you do this?!
Wait, before you—
You opened some stranger's mail and you didn't even show me?! What did it say?!
BEN LELAND
926 ROSITA AVE
PACIFICA CA 94044
SARAH RICHARDSAN
741 TELEGRAPH AVE
OAKLAND CA 94606
SARAH RICHARSON
741 TELEGRAPH AVE
OAKLAND CA 94606
Oh, my God... This is all within the last two months?
Go ahead, read one of 'em!
Oh, man, this is so wrong...
You wanna know "wrong"? Read one of the letters.
Which is the first one?
It doesn't matter. They're all pretty much the same.
Dearest Sarah,
This morning I cut myself shaving. When the blood dribbled into my mouth, it reminded me of the taste of your tears. When I hear the soft murmur of a stream, it's your voice that whispers to me. When I slip my hands over a silk sheet, it's your back that I caress. When my head hits the pillow at night, it's onto your heavenly bosom that I rest.
I wonder... Do you hear me breathing next to you when you open a window against the breeze? Do you feel your pulse race every time you close your
Ha ha ha! Is this for real?!
I'm afraid he's being completely sincere. And I really think this Sarah person moved away just to eliminate all connections with this guy.

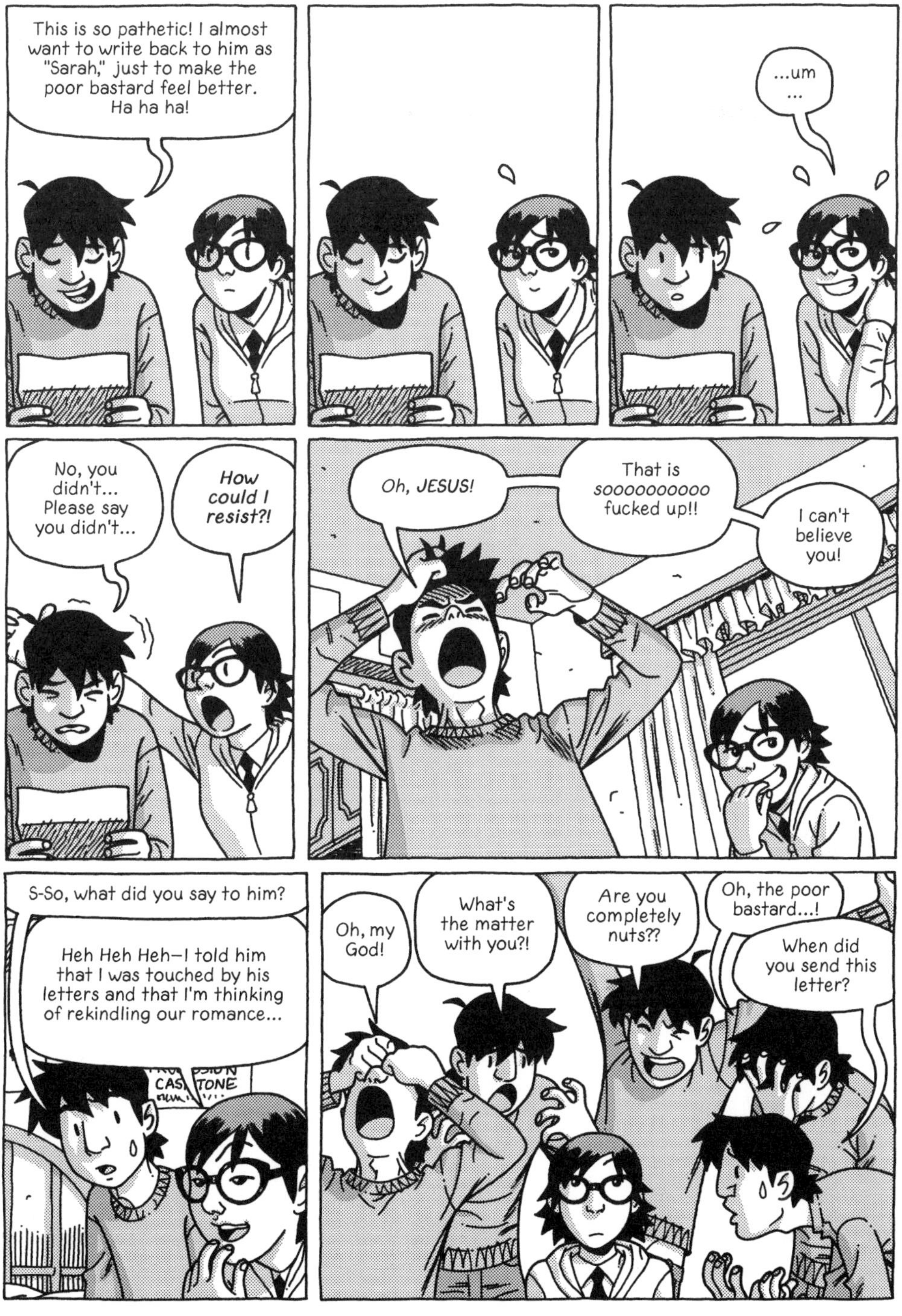
This is so pathetic! I almost want to write back to him as "Sarah," just to make the poor bastard feel better. Ha ha ha!
...um ...
No, you didn't... Please say you didn't...
How could I resist?!
Oh, JESUS!
That is soooooooooo fucked up!!
I can't believe you!
S-So, what did you say to him?
Heh Heh Heh—I told him that I was touched by his letters and that I'm thinking of rekindling our romance...
Oh, my God!
What's the matter with you?!
Are you completely nuts??
Oh, the poor bastard...!
When did you send this letter?

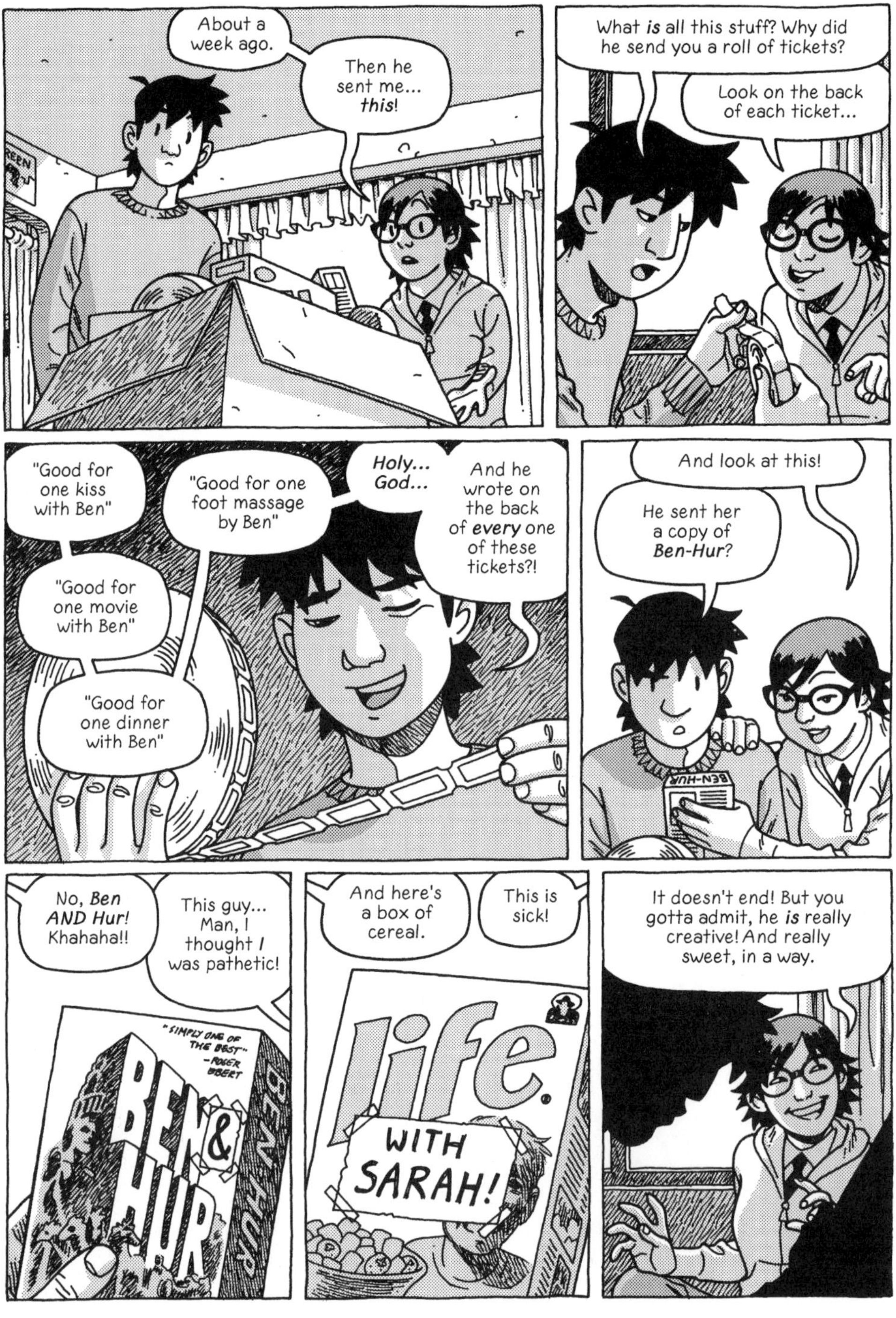
About a week ago.
Then he sent me... *this*!
What *is* all this stuff? Why did he send you a roll of tickets?
Look on the back of each ticket...
"Good for one kiss with Ben"
"Good for one movie with Ben"
"Good for one dinner with Ben"
"Good for one foot massage by Ben"
Holy... God...
And he wrote on the back of *every* one of these tickets?!
And look at this!
He sent her a copy of *Ben-Hur*?
BEN-HUR
No, *Ben AND Hur*! Khahaha!!
This guy... Man, I thought *I* was pathetic!
"SIMPLY ONE OF THE BEST" —ROGER EBERT
BEN & HUR
BEN HUR
And here's a box of cereal.
This is sick!
life.
WITH SARAH!
It doesn't end! But you gotta admit, he *is* really creative! And really sweet, in a way.

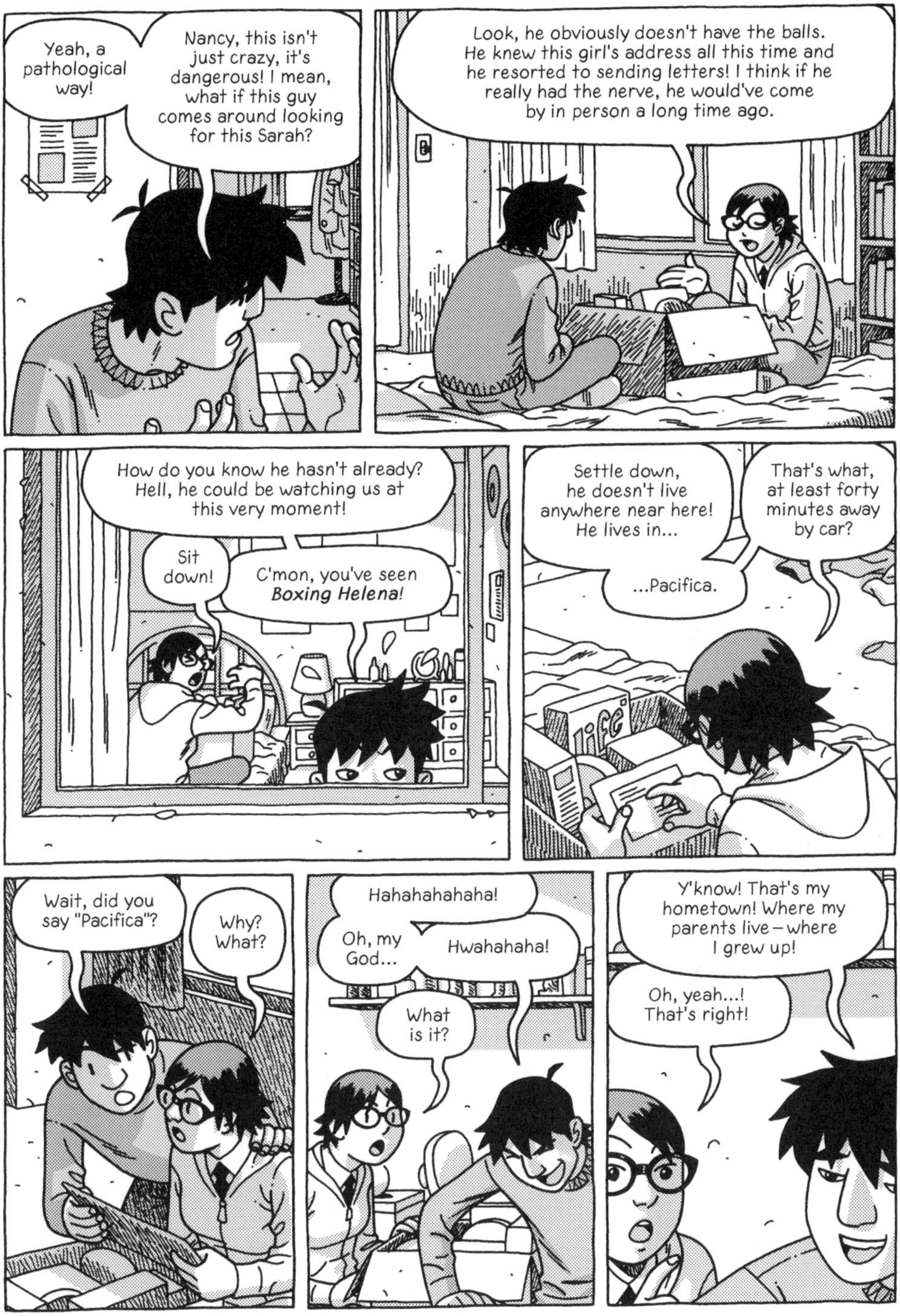

Yeah, a pathological way!
Nancy, this isn't just crazy, it's dangerous! I mean, what if this guy comes around looking for this Sarah?
Look, he obviously doesn't have the balls. He knew this girl's address all this time and he resorted to sending letters! I think if he really had the nerve, he would've come by in person a long time ago.
How do you know he hasn't already? Hell, he could be watching us at this very moment!
Sit down!
C'mon, you've seen *Boxing Helena*!
Settle down, he doesn't live anywhere near here! He lives in...
...Pacifica.
That's what, at least forty minutes away by car?
Wait, did you say "Pacifica"?
Why? What?
Hahahahahaha!
Oh, my God...
Hwahahaha!
What is it?
Y'know! That's my hometown! Where my parents live—where I grew up!
Oh, yeah...! That's right!

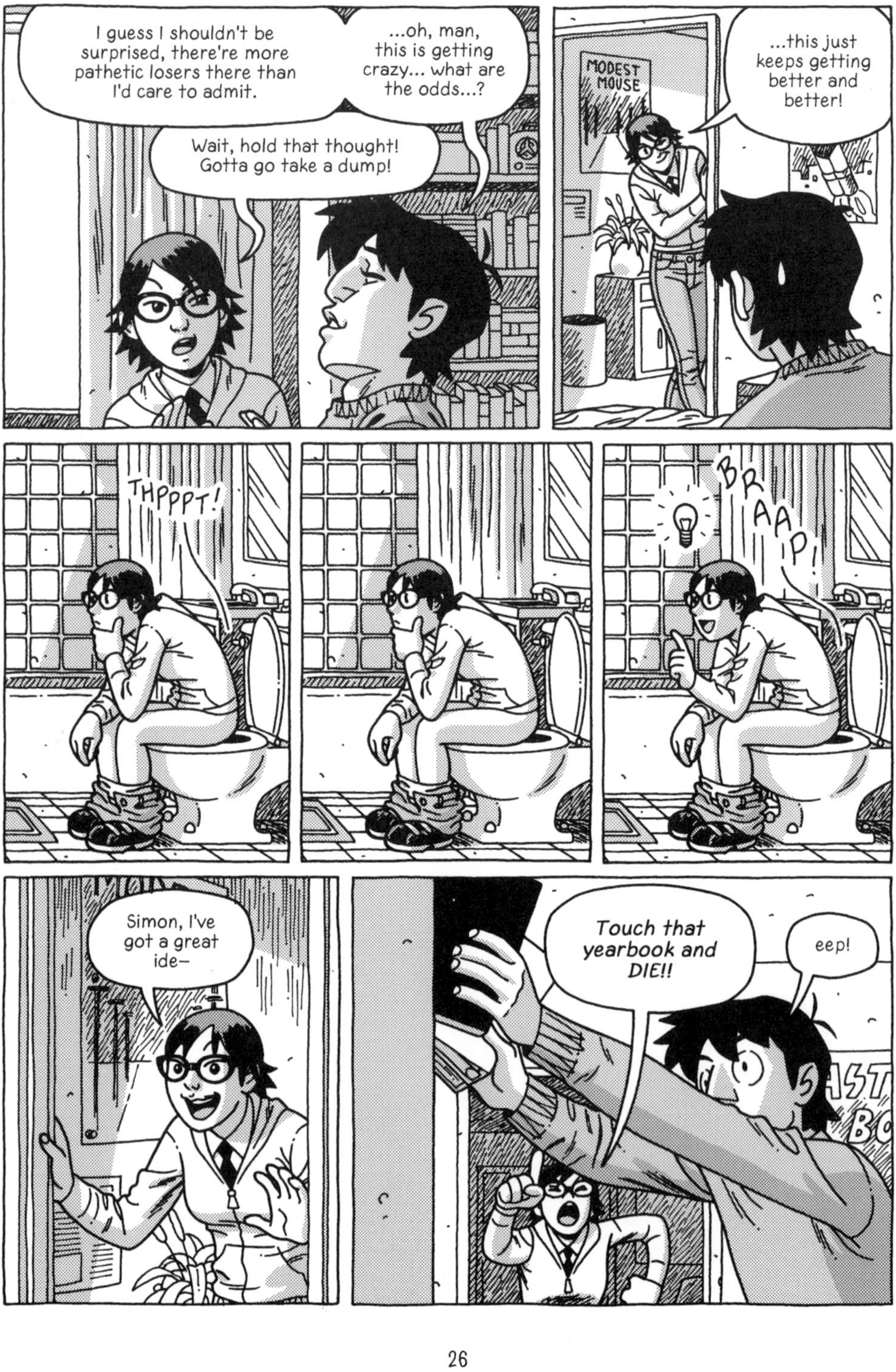
I guess I shouldn't be surprised, there're more pathetic losers there than I'd care to admit.
...oh, man, this is getting crazy... what are the odds...?
Wait, hold that thought! Gotta go take a dump!
MODEST MOUSE
...this just keeps getting better and better!
THPPPT!
BRAAP!
Simon, I've got a great ide–
Touch that yearbook and DIE!!
eep!

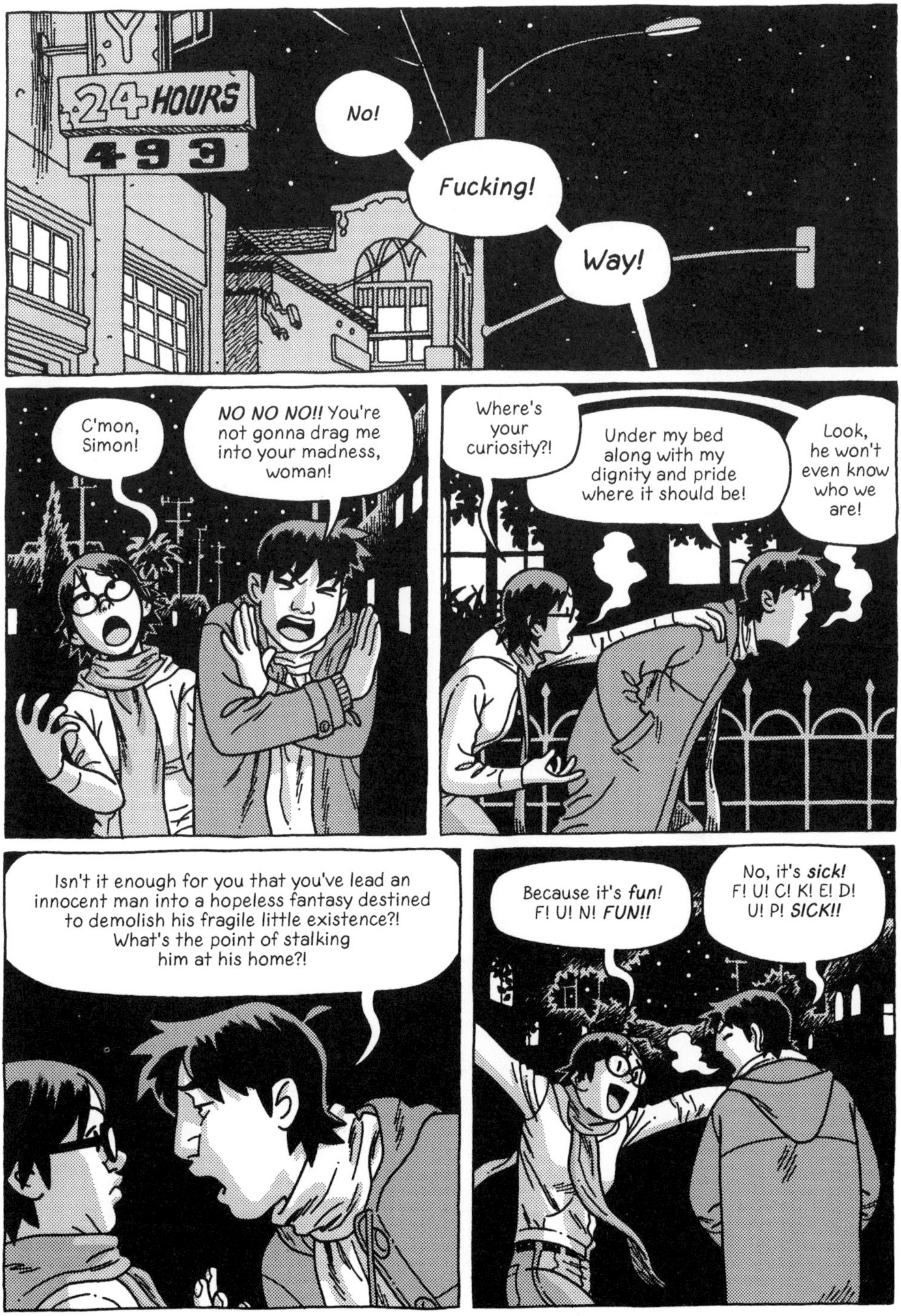
24 HOURS
493
No!
Fucking!
Way!
C'mon, Simon!
NO NO NO!! You're not gonna drag me into your madness, woman!
Where's your curiosity?!
Under my bed along with my dignity and pride where it should be!
Look, he won't even know who we are!
Isn't it enough for you that you've lead an innocent man into a hopeless fantasy destined to demolish his fragile little existence?! What's the point of stalking him at his home?!
Because it's *fun!* F! U! N! ***FUN!!***
No, it's ***sick!*** F! U! C! K! E! D! U! P! ***SICK!!***

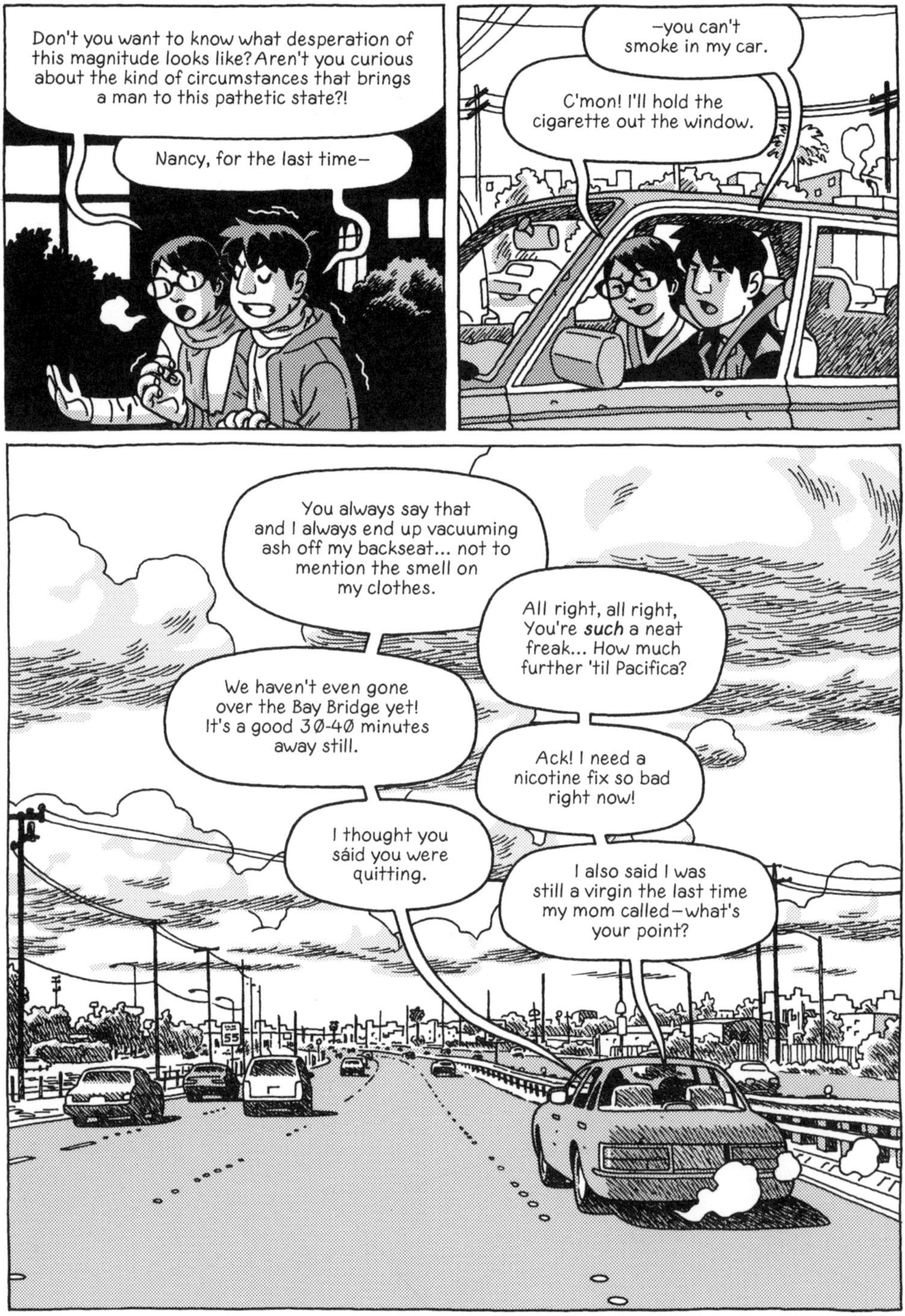

Don't you want to know what desperation of this magnitude looks like? Aren't you curious about the kind of circumstances that brings a man to this pathetic state?!
Nancy, for the last time–
–you can't smoke in my car.
C'mon! I'll hold the cigarette out the window.
You always say that and I always end up vacuuming ash off my backseat... not to mention the smell on my clothes.
All right, all right, You're *such* a neat freak... How much further 'til Pacifica?
We haven't even gone over the Bay Bridge yet! It's a good 30-40 minutes away still.
Ack! I need a nicotine fix so bad right now!
I thought you said you were quitting.
I also said I was still a virgin the last time my mom called–what's your point?
55

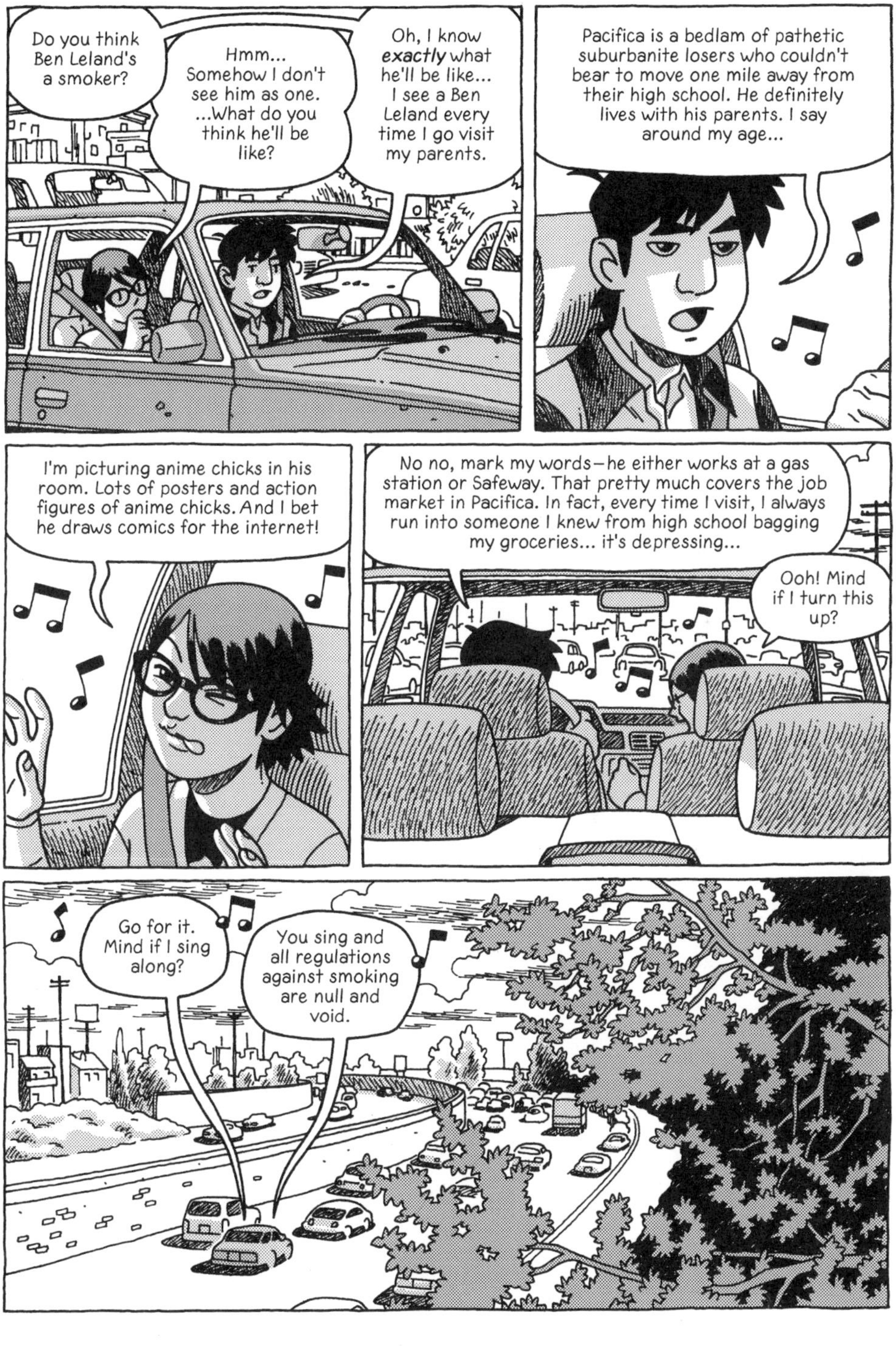
Do you think Ben Leland's a smoker?
Hmm... Somehow I don't see him as one. ...What do you think he'll be like?
Oh, I know *exactly* what he'll be like... I see a Ben Leland every time I go visit my parents.
Pacifica is a bedlam of pathetic suburbanite losers who couldn't bear to move one mile away from their high school. He definitely lives with his parents. I say around my age...
I'm picturing anime chicks in his room. Lots of posters and action figures of anime chicks. And I bet he draws comics for the internet!
No no, mark my words—he either works at a gas station or Safeway. That pretty much covers the job market in Pacifica. In fact, every time I visit, I always run into someone I knew from high school bagging my groceries... it's depressing...
Ooh! Mind if I turn this up?
Go for it. Mind if I sing along?
You sing and all regulations against smoking are null and void.

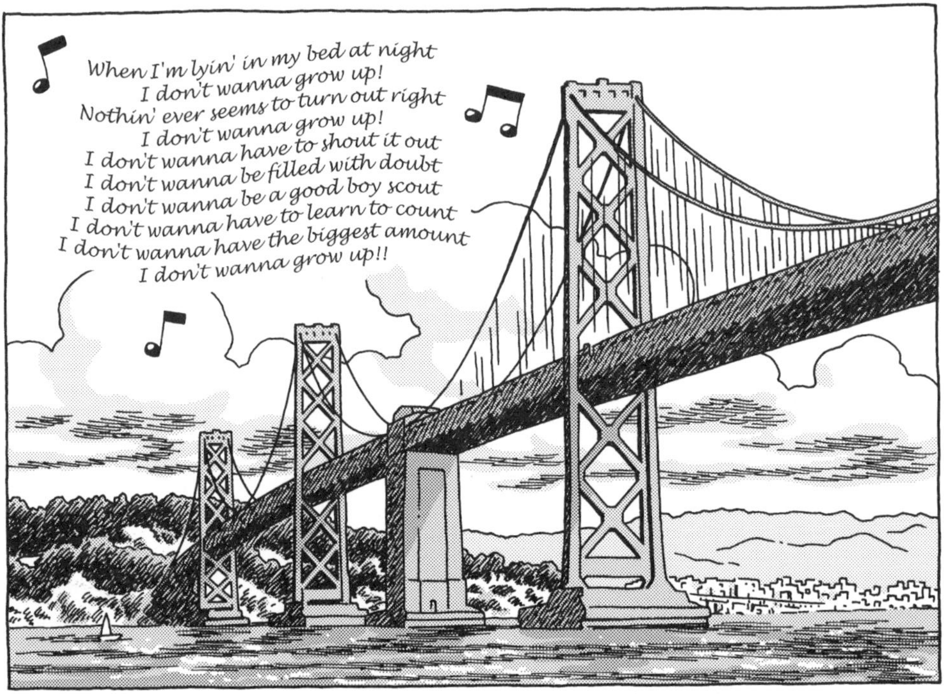
When I'm lyin' in my bed at night
I don't wanna grow up!
Nothin' ever seems to turn out right
I don't wanna grow up!
I don't wanna have to shout it out
I don't wanna be filled with doubt
I don't wanna be a good boy scout
I don't wanna have to learn to count
I don't wanna have the biggest amount
I don't wanna grow up!!

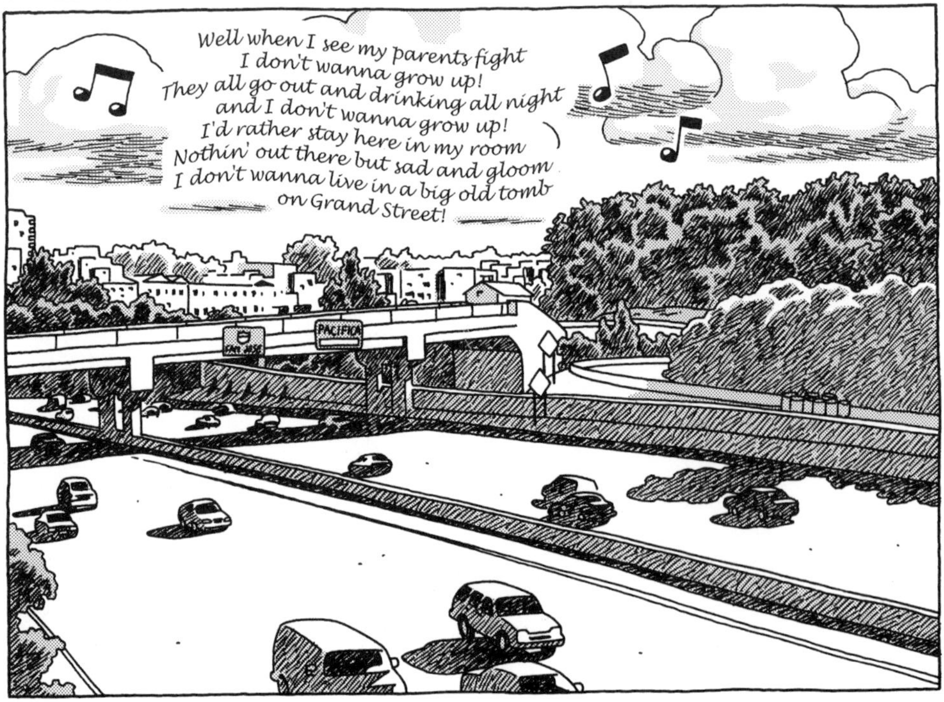
Well when I see my parents fight
I don't wanna grow up!
They all go out and drinking all night
and I don't wanna grow up!
I'd rather stay here in my room
Nothin' out there but sad and gloom
I don't wanna live in a big old tomb
on Grand Street!
PACIFICA
SAN JOSE

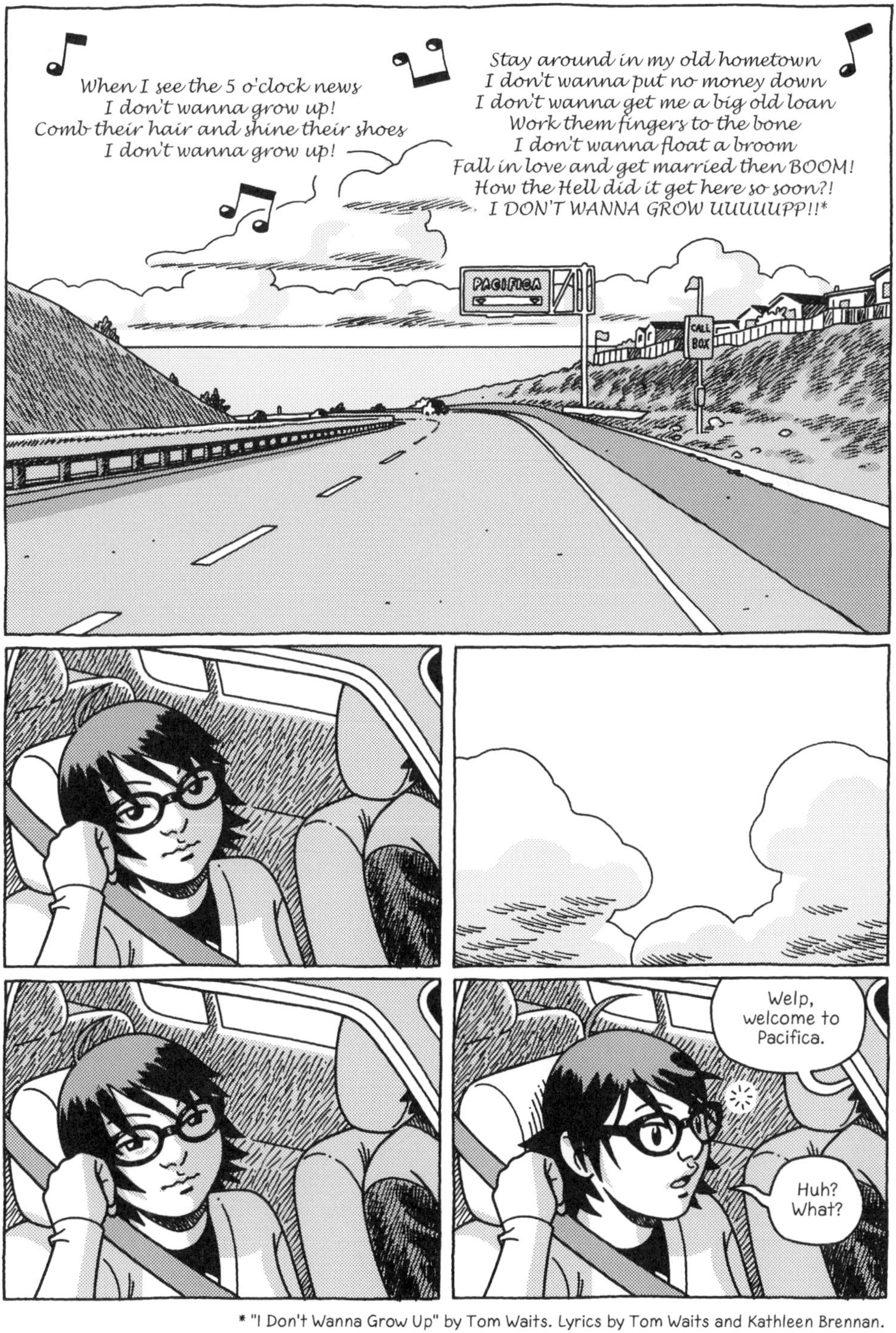
When I see the 5 o'clock news
I don't wanna grow up!
Comb their hair and shine their shoes
I don't wanna grow up!
Stay around in my old hometown
I don't wanna put no money down
I don't wanna get me a big old loan
Work them fingers to the bone
I don't wanna float a broom
Fall in love and get married then BOOM!
How the Hell did it get here so soon?!
I DON'T WANNA GROW UUUUUPP!!*
PACIFICA
CALL BOX
Welp, welcome to Pacifica.
Huh? What?

* "I Don't Wanna Grow Up" by Tom Waits. Lyrics by Tom Waits and Kathleen Brennan.

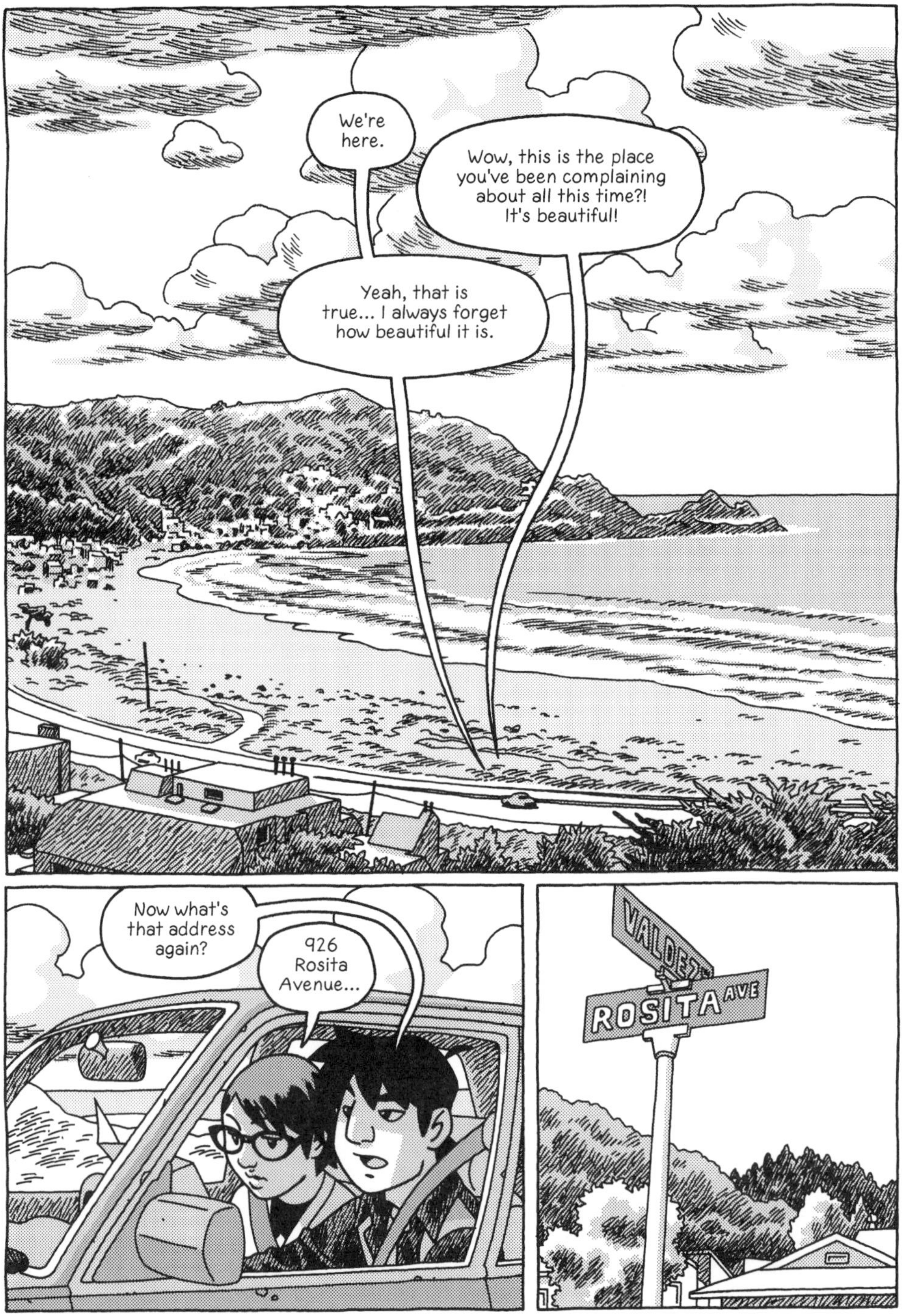
We're here.
Wow, this is the place you've been complaining about all this time?! It's beautiful!
Yeah, that is true... I always forget how beautiful it is.
Now what's that address again?
926 Rosita Avenue...
ROSITA AVE

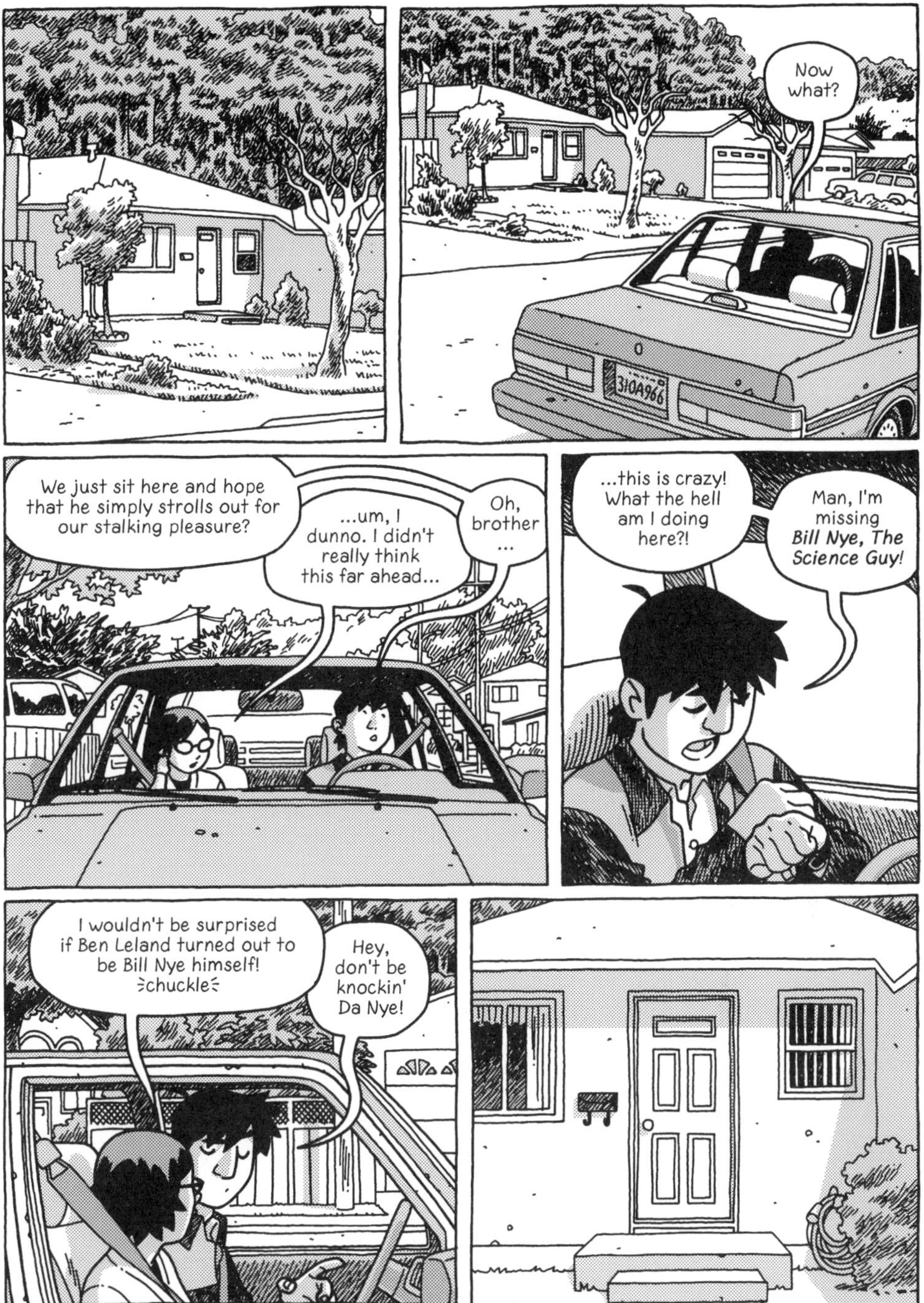
Now what?
310A966
We just sit here and hope that he simply strolls out for our stalking pleasure?
...um, I dunno. I didn't really think this far ahead...
Oh, brother...
...this is crazy! What the hell am I doing here?!
Man, I'm missing *Bill Nye, The Science Guy!*
I wouldn't be surprised if Ben Leland turned out to be Bill Nye himself! ⋛chuckle⋚
Hey, don't be knockin' Da Nye!

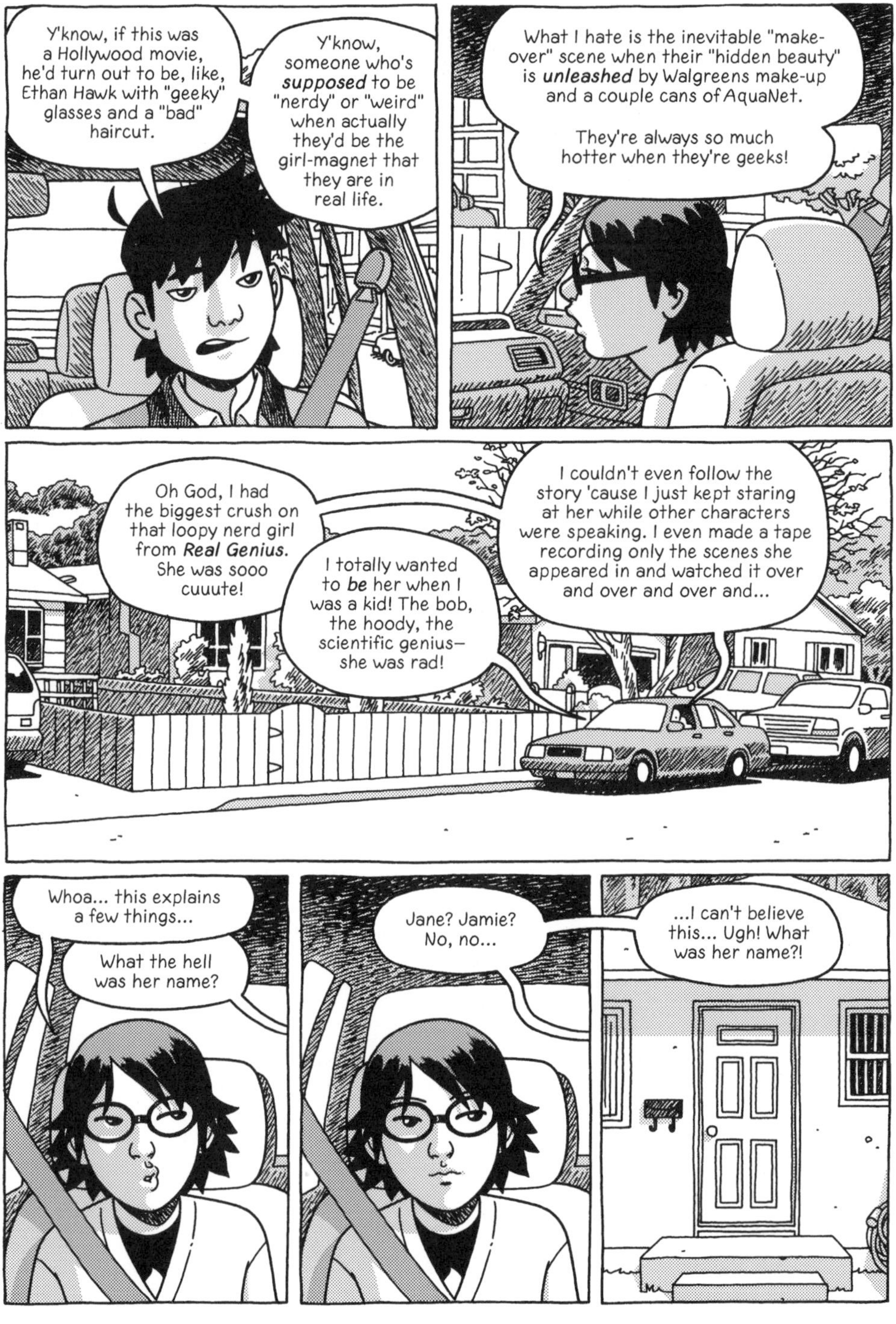

Y'know, if this was a Hollywood movie, he'd turn out to be, like, Ethan Hawk with "geeky" glasses and a "bad" haircut.
Y'know, someone who's *supposed* to be "nerdy" or "weird" when actually they'd be the girl-magnet that they are in real life.
What I hate is the inevitable "make-over" scene when their "hidden beauty" is *unleashed* by Walgreens make-up and a couple cans of AquaNet.
They're always so much hotter when they're geeks!
Oh God, I had the biggest crush on that loopy nerd girl from *Real Genius*. She was sooo cuuute!
I totally wanted to *be* her when I was a kid! The bob, the hoody, the scientific genius– she was rad!
I couldn't even follow the story 'cause I just kept staring at her while other characters were speaking. I even made a tape recording only the scenes she appeared in and watched it over and over and over and...
Whoa... this explains a few things...
What the hell was her name?
Jane? Jamie? No, no...
...I can't believe this... Ugh! What was her name?!

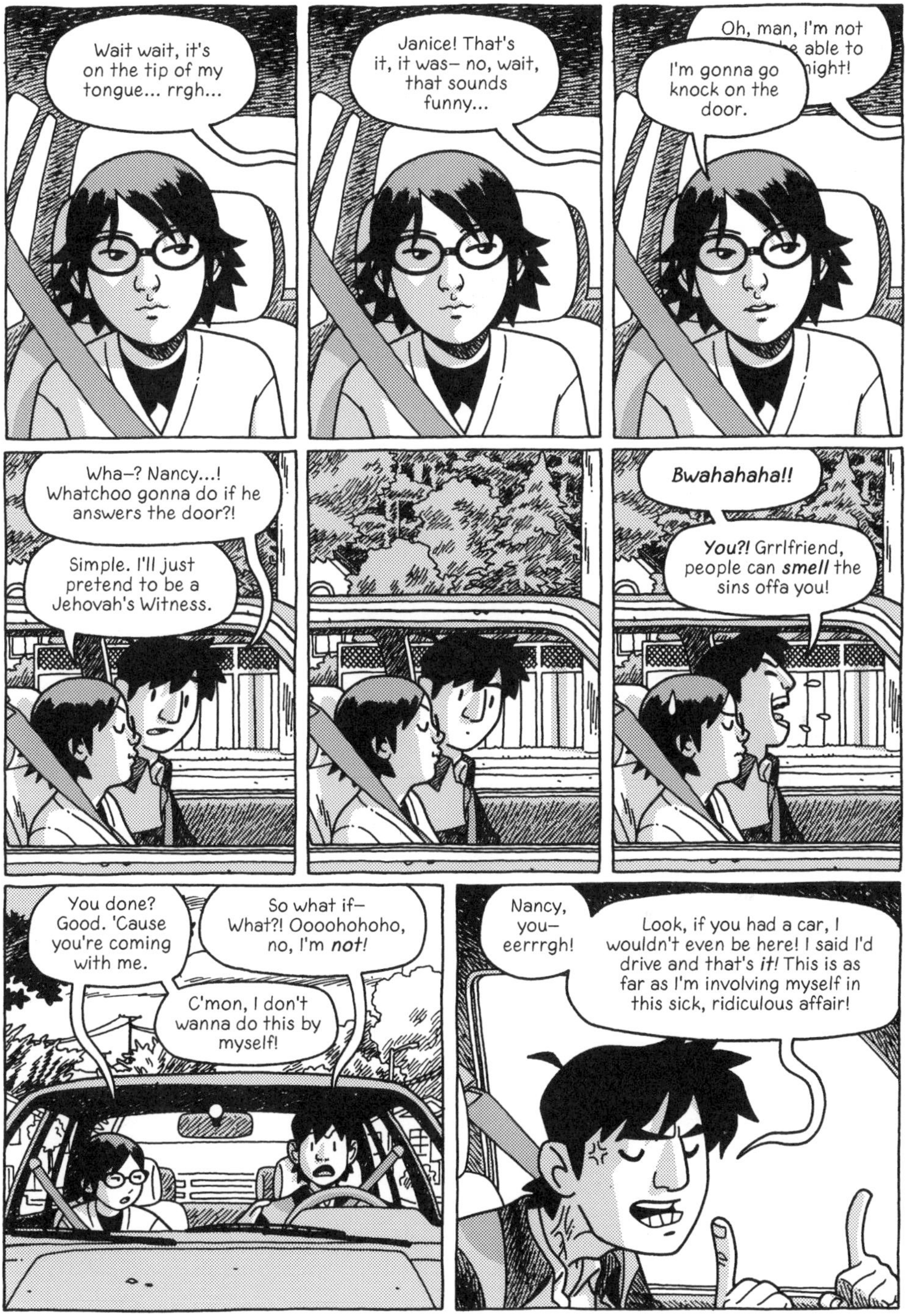

Wait wait, it's on the tip of my tongue... rrgh...
Janice! That's it, it was– no, wait, that sounds funny...
Oh, man, I'm not
able to
night!
I'm gonna go knock on the door.
Wha–? Nancy...! Whatchoo gonna do if he answers the door?!
Simple. I'll just pretend to be a Jehovah's Witness.
Bwahahaha!!
You?! Grrlfriend, people can ***smell*** the sins offa you!
You done? Good. 'Cause you're coming with me.
So what if– What?! Ooooohohoho, no, I'm ***not!***
C'mon, I don't wanna do this by myself!
Nancy, you– eerrrgh!
Look, if you had a car, I wouldn't even be here! I said I'd drive and that's *it!* This is as far as I'm involving myself in this sick, ridiculous affair!

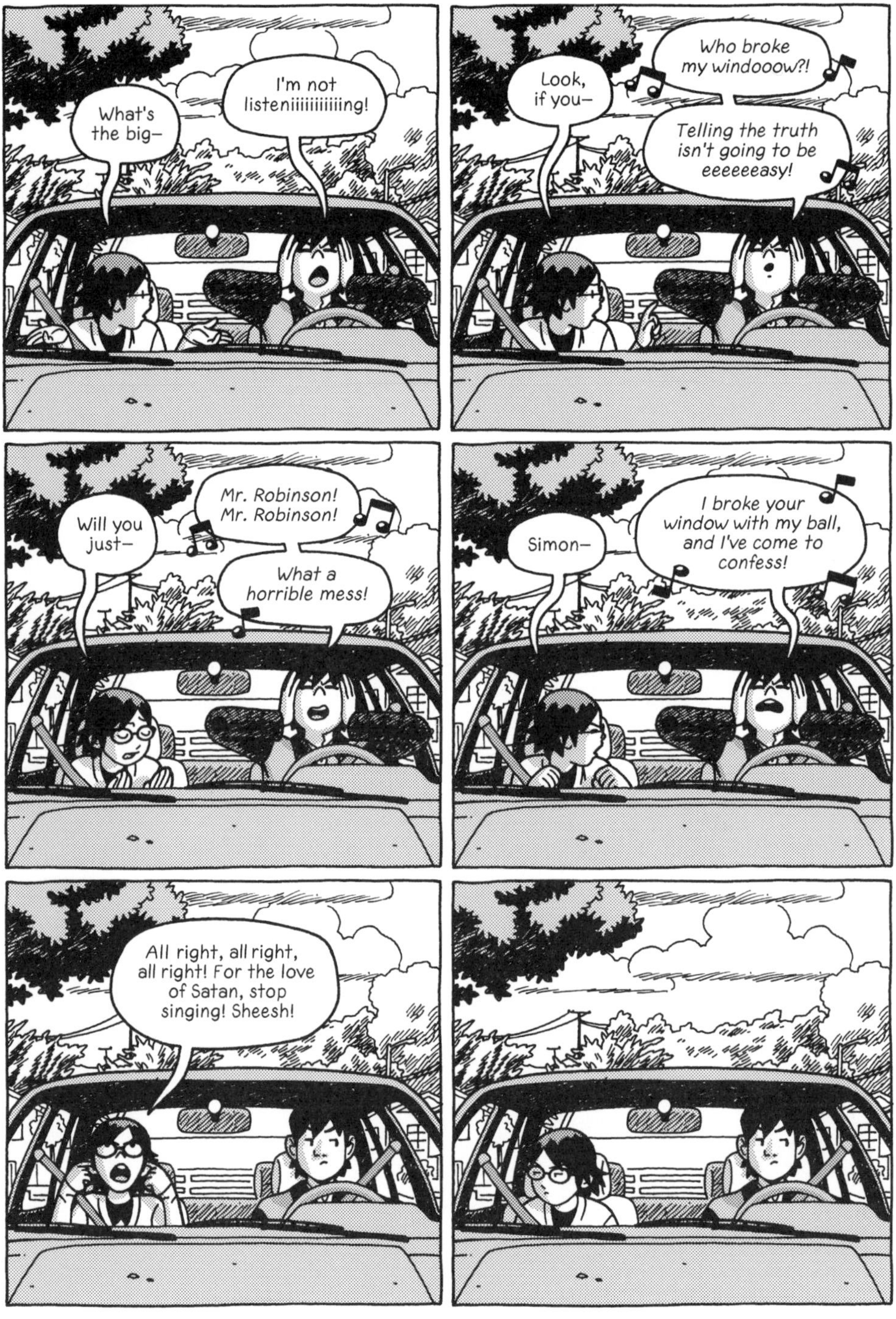
What's the big–
I'm not listeniiiiiiiiiiiing!
Look, if you–
Who broke my windooow?!
Telling the truth isn't going to be eeeeeeasy!
Will you just–
Mr. Robinson! Mr. Robinson!
What a horrible mess!
Simon–
I broke your window with my ball, and I've come to confess!
All right, all right, all right! For the love of Satan, stop singing! Sheesh!

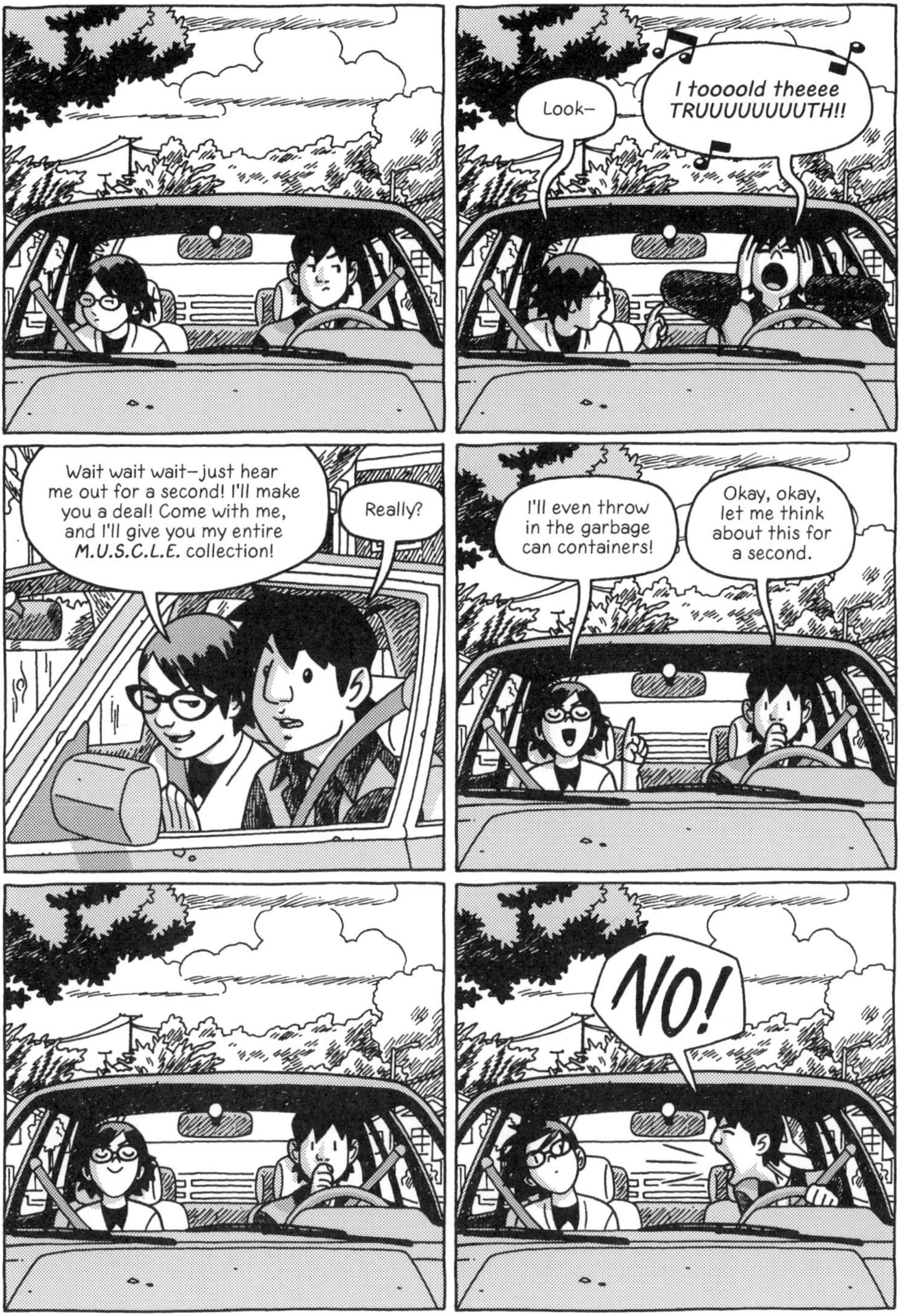
Look–
I tooooold theeee TRUUUUUUUUTH!!
Wait wait wait–just hear me out for a second! I'll make you a deal! Come with me, and I'll give you my entire *M.U.S.C.L.E.* collection!
Really?
I'll even throw in the garbage can containers!
Okay, okay, let me think about this for a second.
NO!

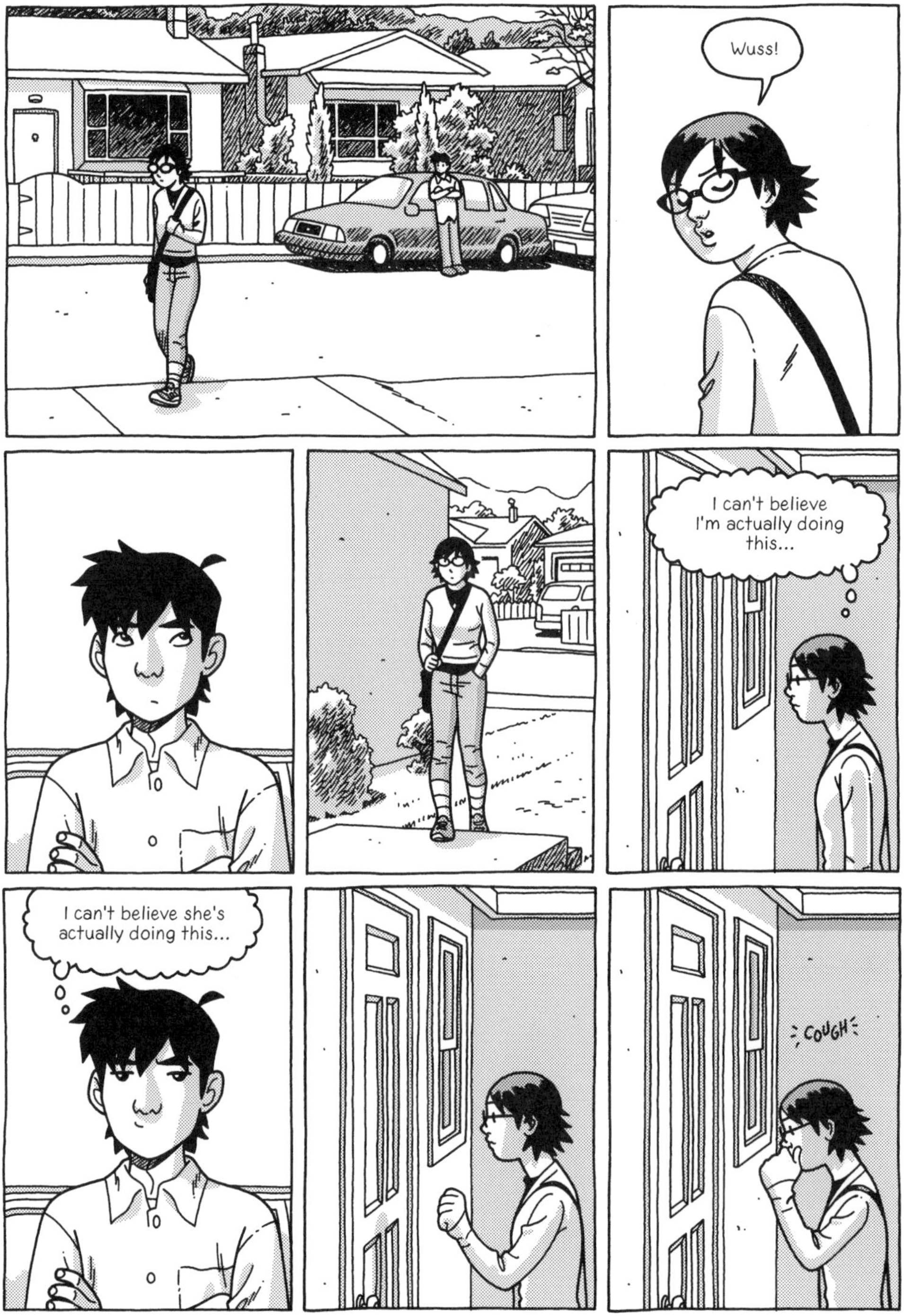
Wuss!
I can't believe I'm actually doing this...
I can't believe she's actually doing this...
COUGH

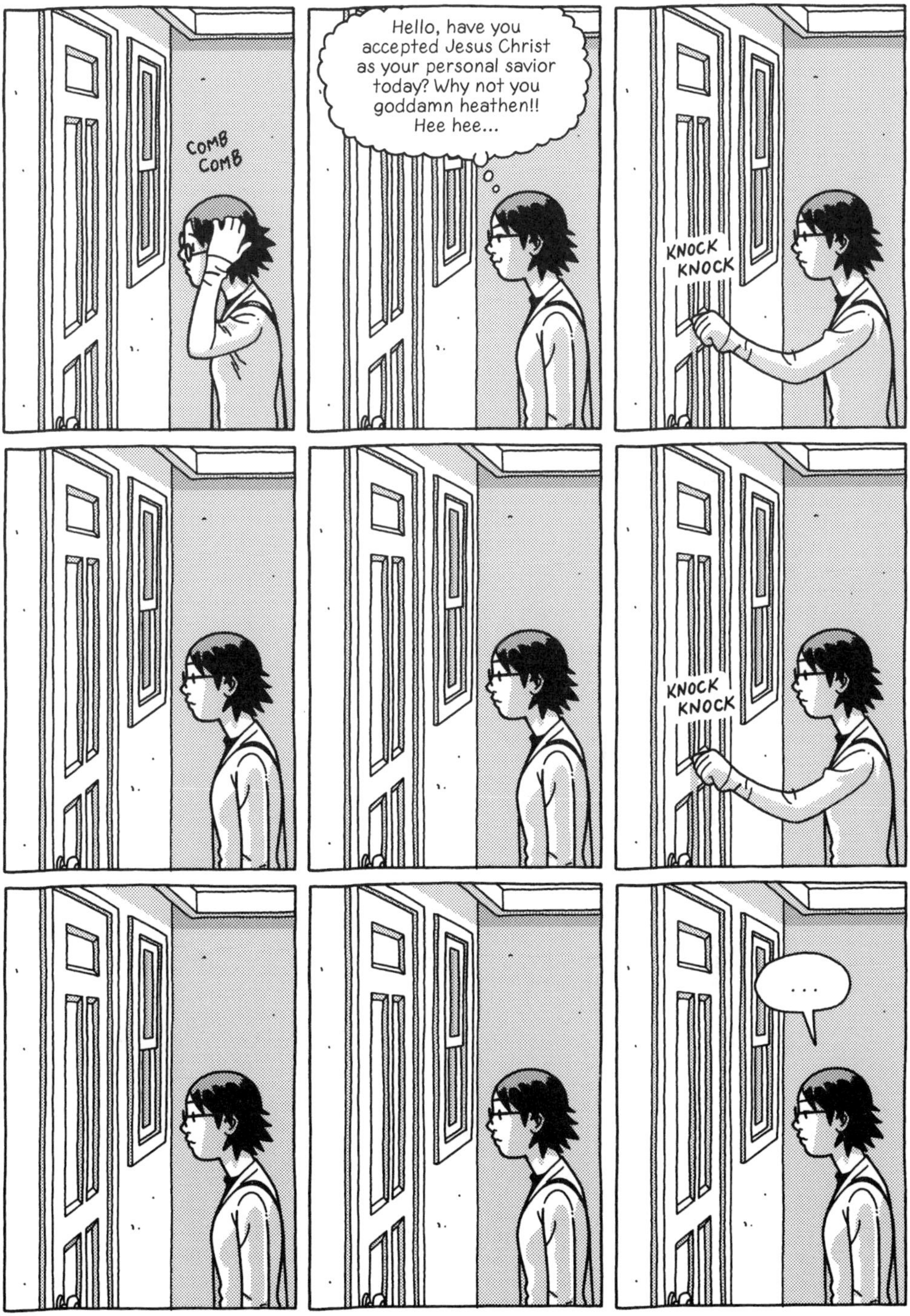
COMB COMB
Hello, have you accepted Jesus Christ as your personal savior today? Why not you goddamn heathen!! Hee hee...
KNOCK KNOCK
KNOCK KNOCK
. . .

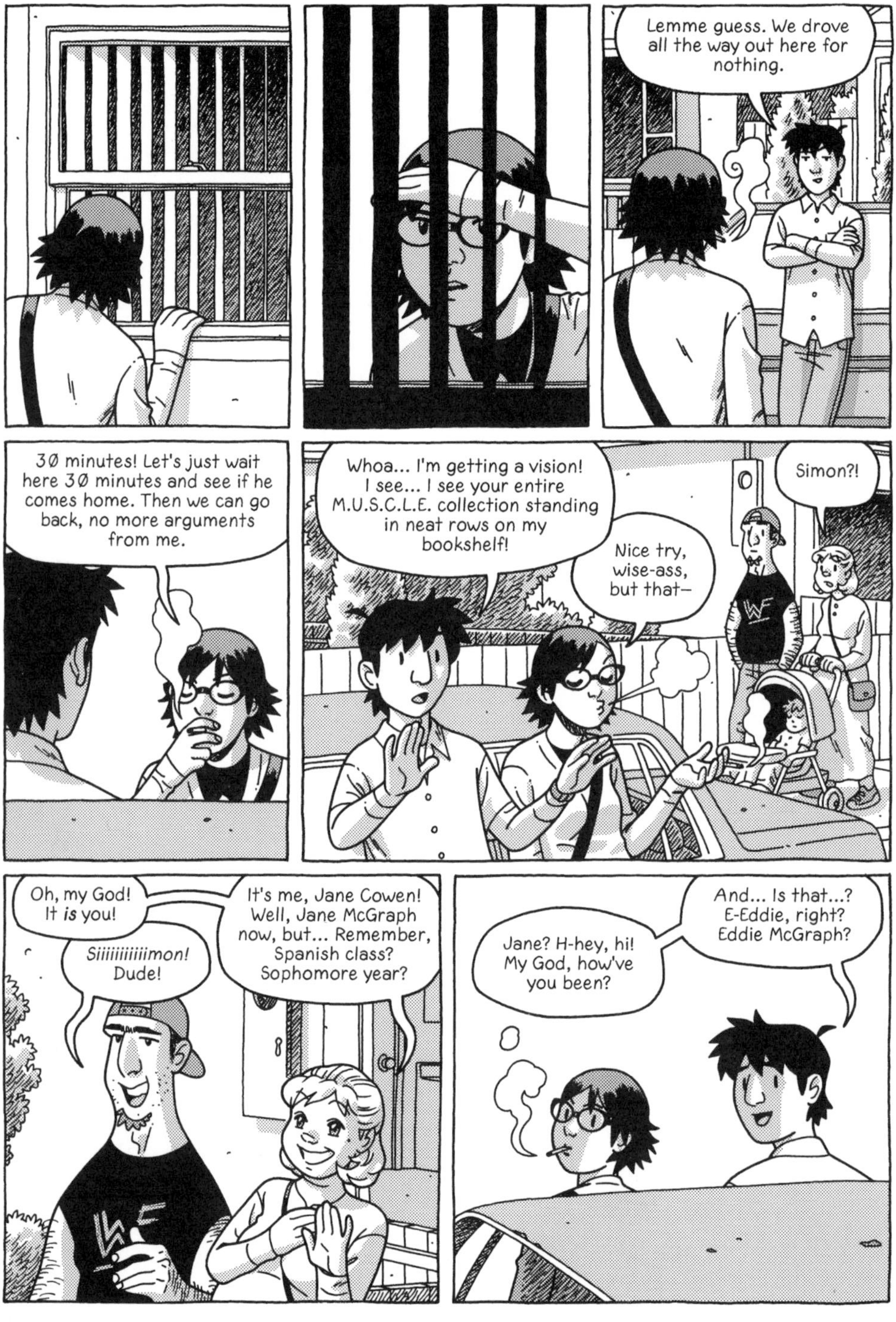
Lemme guess. We drove all the way out here for nothing.
30 minutes! Let's just wait here 30 minutes and see if he comes home. Then we can go back, no more arguments from me.
Whoa... I'm getting a vision! I see... I see your entire M.U.S.C.L.E. collection standing in neat rows on my bookshelf!
Nice try, wise-ass, but that–
Simon?!
Oh, my God! It *is* you!
Siiiiiiiiiimon! Dude!
It's me, Jane Cowen! Well, Jane McGraph now, but... Remember, Spanish class? Sophomore year?
Jane? H-hey, hi! My God, how've you been?
And... Is that...? E-Eddie, right? Eddie McGraph?

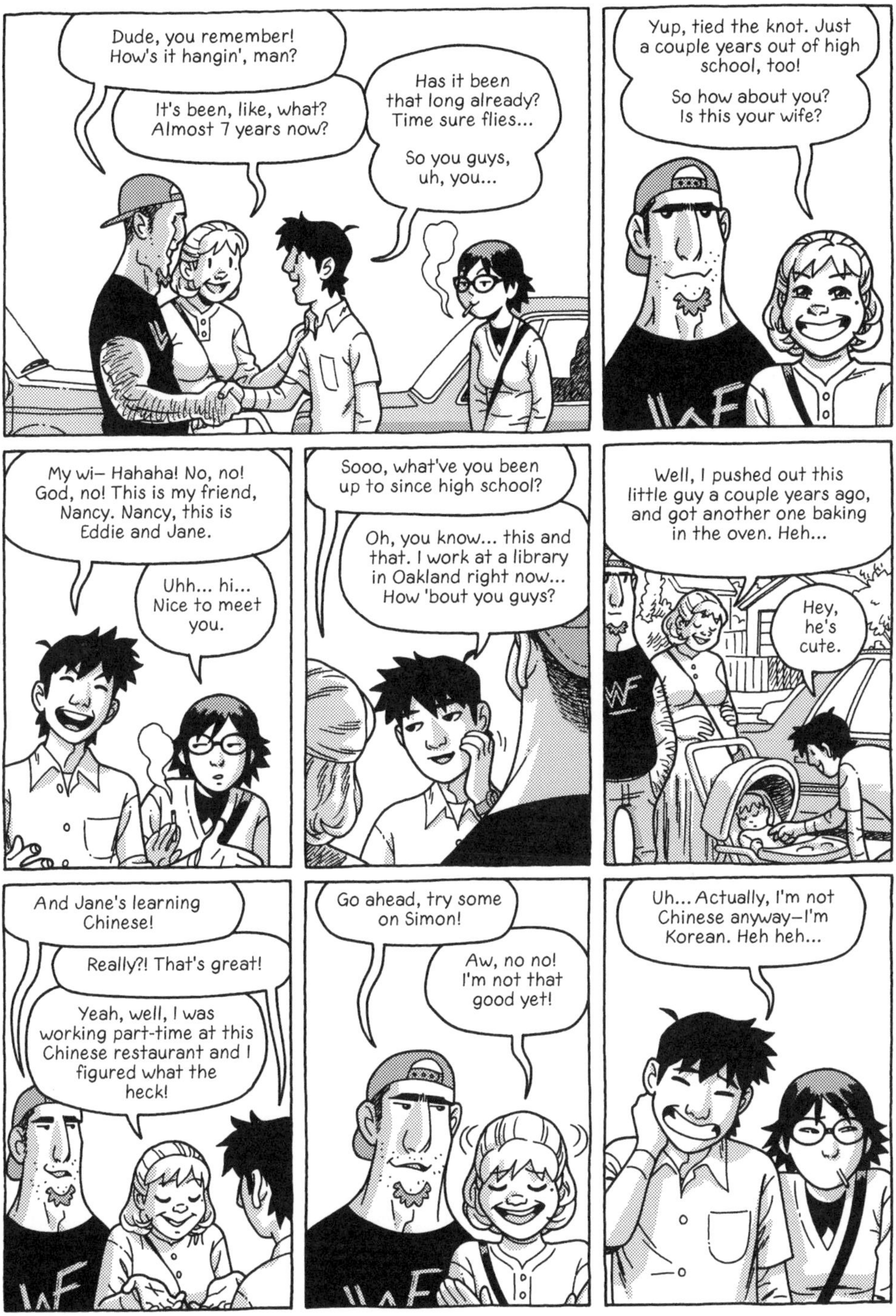

Dude, you remember! How's it hangin', man?
It's been, like, what? Almost 7 years now?
Has it been that long already? Time sure flies...
So you guys, uh, you...
Yup, tied the knot. Just a couple years out of high school, too!
So how about you? Is this your wife?
My wi– Hahaha! No, no! God, no! This is my friend, Nancy. Nancy, this is Eddie and Jane.
Uhh... hi... Nice to meet you.
Sooo, what've you been up to since high school?
Oh, you know... this and that. I work at a library in Oakland right now... How 'bout you guys?
Well, I pushed out this little guy a couple years ago, and got another one baking in the oven. Heh...
Hey, he's cute.
And Jane's learning Chinese!
Really?! That's great!
Yeah, well, I was working part-time at this Chinese restaurant and I figured what the heck!
Go ahead, try some on Simon!
Aw, no no! I'm not that good yet!
Uh... Actually, I'm not Chinese anyway—I'm Korean. Heh heh...

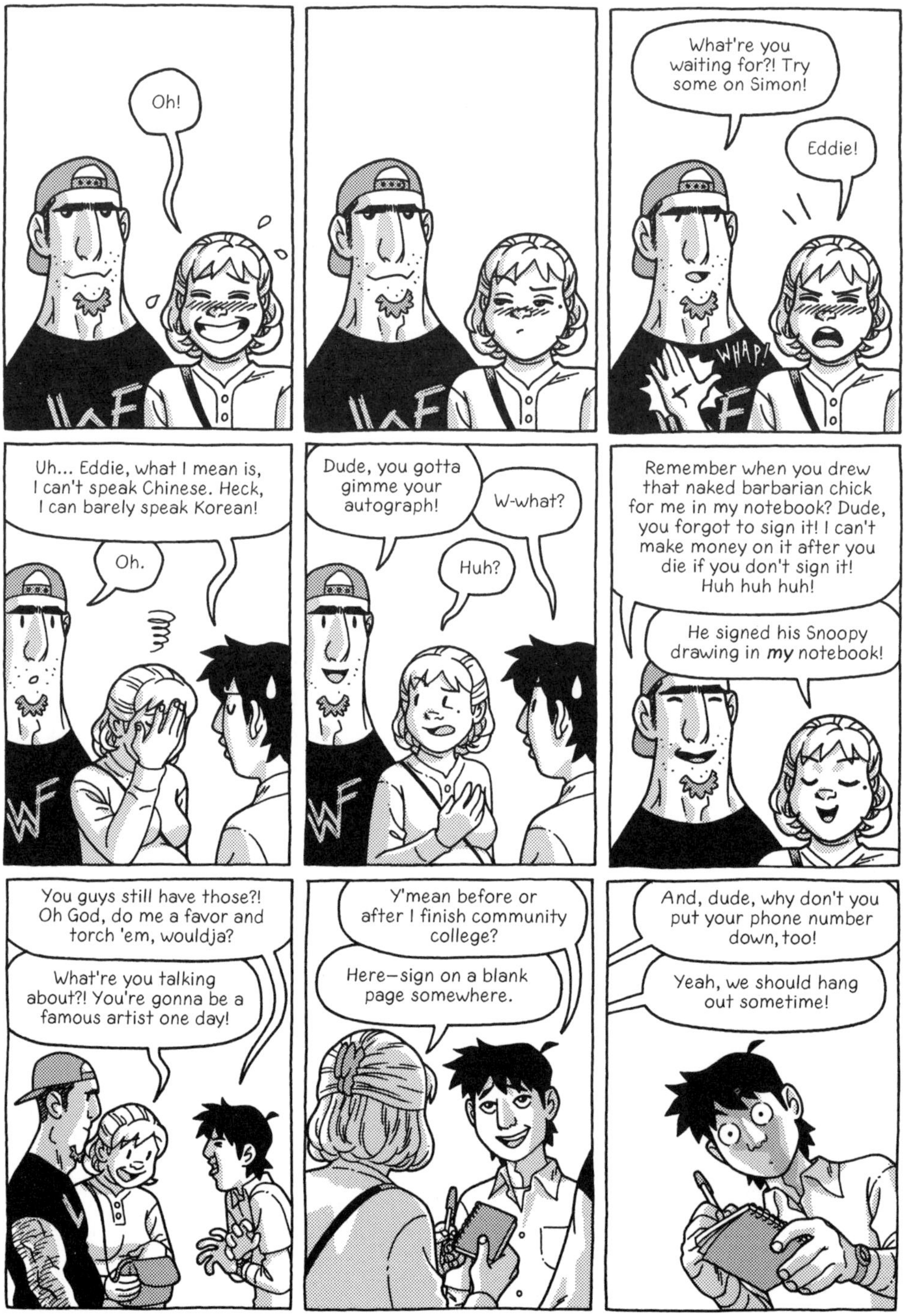
Oh!
What're you waiting for?! Try some on Simon!
Eddie!
WHAP!
Uh... Eddie, what I mean is, I can't speak Chinese. Heck, I can barely speak Korean!
Oh.
Dude, you gotta gimme your autograph!
W-what?
Huh?
Remember when you drew that naked barbarian chick for me in my notebook? Dude, you forgot to sign it! I can't make money on it after you die if you don't sign it! Huh huh huh!
He signed his Snoopy drawing in my notebook!
You guys still have those?! Oh God, do me a favor and torch 'em, wouldja?
What're you talking about?! You're gonna be a famous artist one day!
Y'mean before or after I finish community college?
Here—sign on a blank page somewhere.
And, dude, why don't you put your phone number down, too!
Yeah, we should hang out sometime!

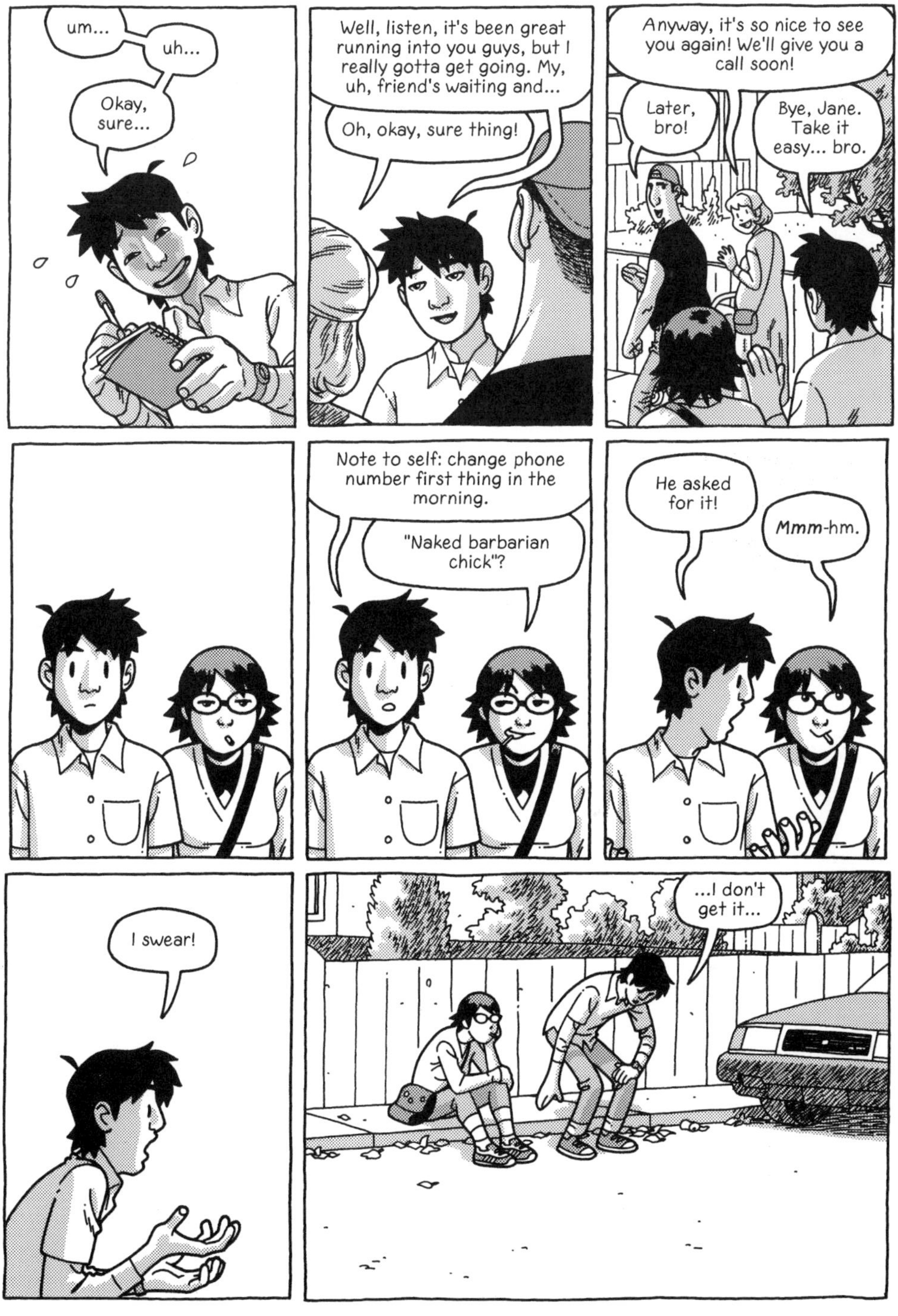
um...
uh...
Okay, sure...
Well, listen, it's been great running into you guys, but I really gotta get going. My, uh, friend's waiting and...
Oh, okay, sure thing!
Anyway, it's so nice to see you again! We'll give you a call soon!
Later, bro!
Bye, Jane. Take it easy... bro.
Note to self: change phone number first thing in the morning.
"Naked barbarian chick"?
He asked for it!
Mmm-hm.
I swear!
...I don't get it...

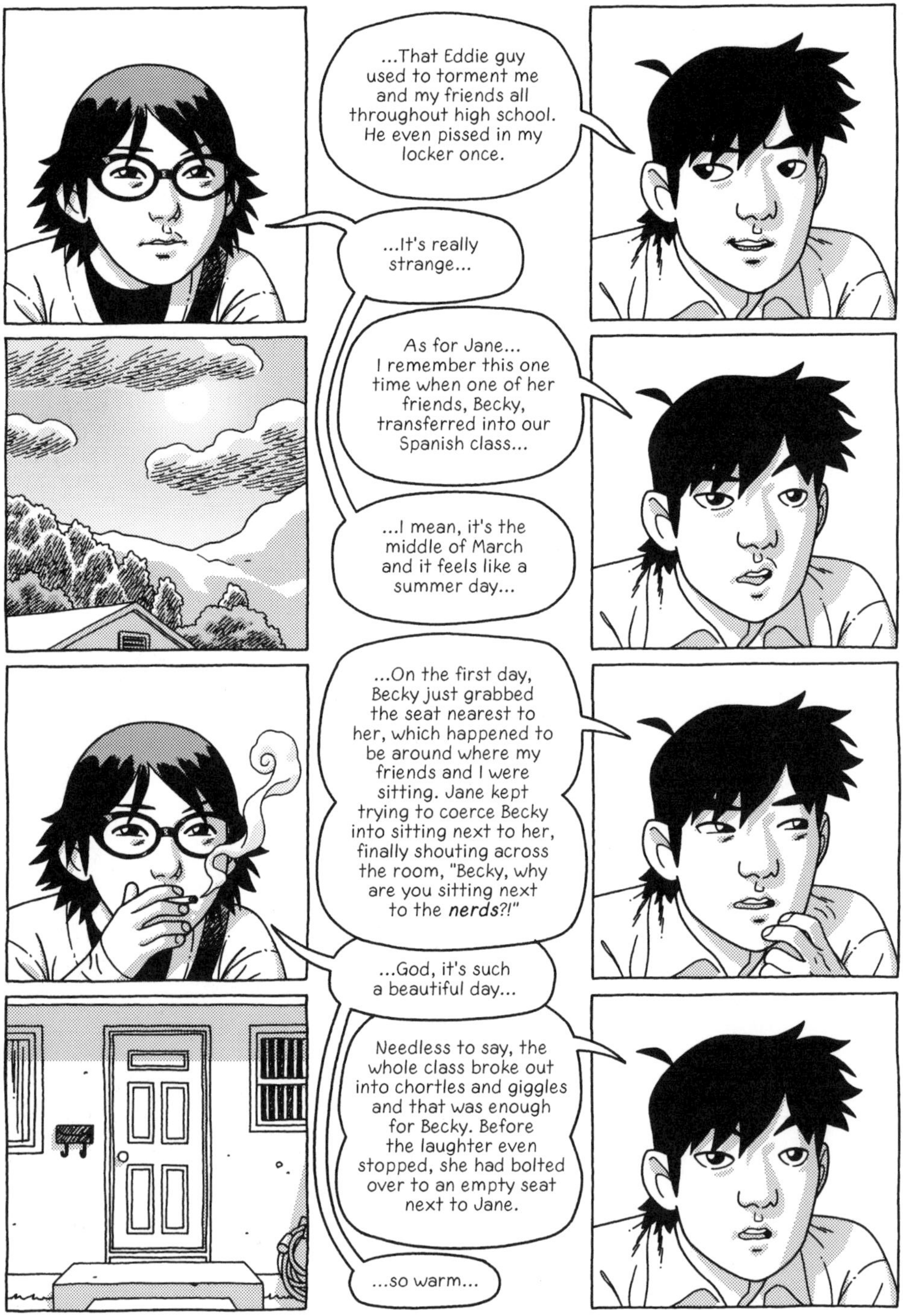

...That Eddie guy used to torment me and my friends all throughout high school. He even pissed in my locker once.
...It's really strange...
As for Jane... I remember this one time when one of her friends, Becky, transferred into our Spanish class...
...I mean, it's the middle of March and it feels like a summer day...
...On the first day, Becky just grabbed the seat nearest to her, which happened to be around where my friends and I were sitting. Jane kept trying to coerce Becky into sitting next to her, finally shouting across the room, "Becky, why are you sitting next to the *nerds?!*"
...God, it's such a beautiful day...
Needless to say, the whole class broke out into chortles and giggles and that was enough for Becky. Before the laughter even stopped, she had bolted over to an empty seat next to Jane.
...so warm...

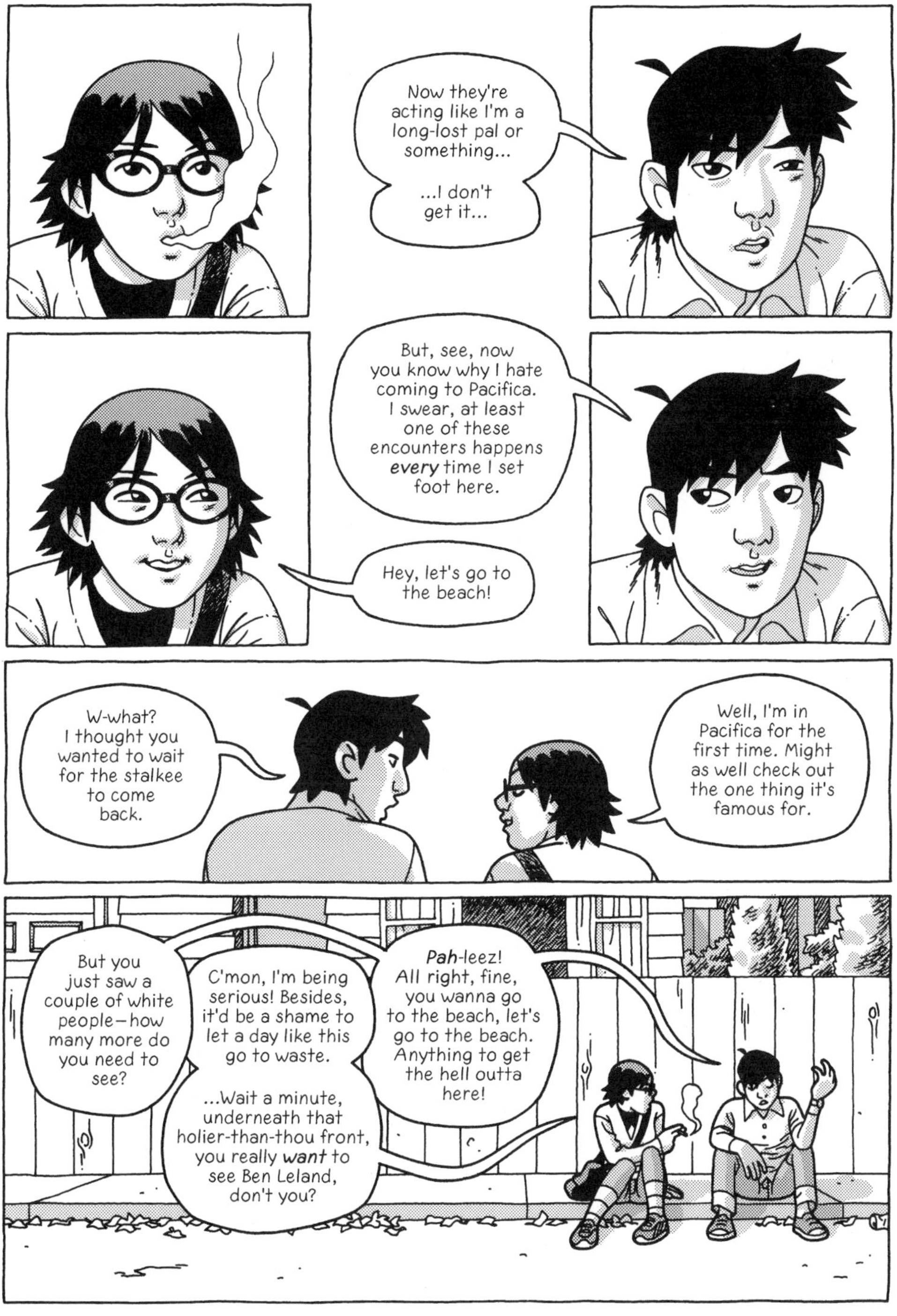
Now they're acting like I'm a long-lost pal or something...
...I don't get it...
But, see, now you know why I hate coming to Pacifica. I swear, at least one of these encounters happens *every* time I set foot here.
Hey, let's go to the beach!
W-what? I thought you wanted to wait for the stalkee to come back.
Well, I'm in Pacifica for the first time. Might as well check out the one thing it's famous for.
But you just saw a couple of white people—how many more do you need to see?
C'mon, I'm being serious! Besides, it'd be a shame to let a day like this go to waste.
...Wait a minute, underneath that holier-than-thou front, you really *want* to see Ben Leland, don't you?
Pah-leez! All right, fine, you wanna go to the beach, let's go to the beach. Anything to get the hell outta here!

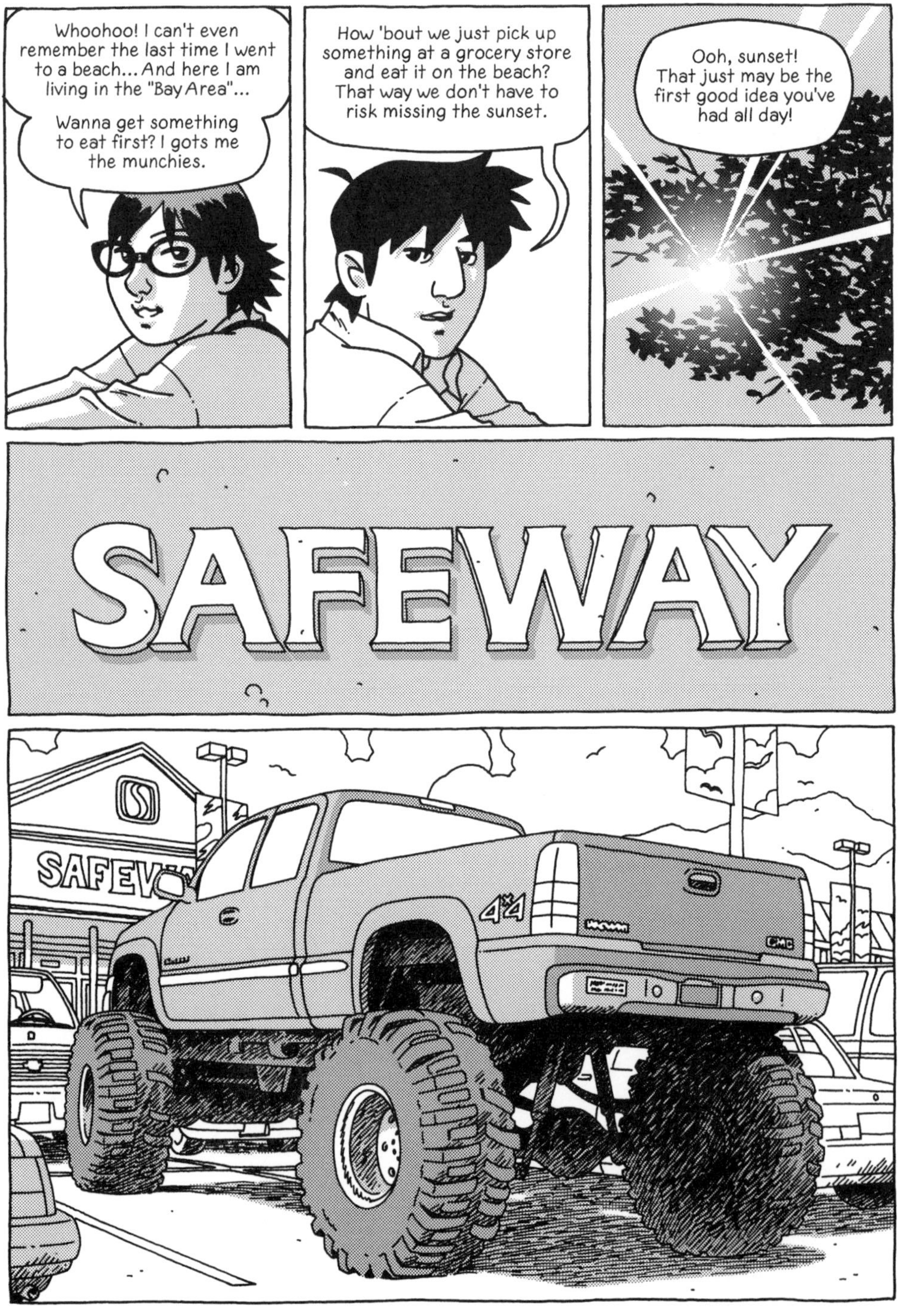
Whoohoo! I can't even remember the last time I went to a beach... And here I am living in the "Bay Area"...
Wanna get something to eat first? I gots me the munchies.
How 'bout we just pick up something at a grocery store and eat it on the beach? That way we don't have to risk missing the sunset.
Ooh, sunset! That just may be the first good idea you've had all day!
SAFEWAY
4x4

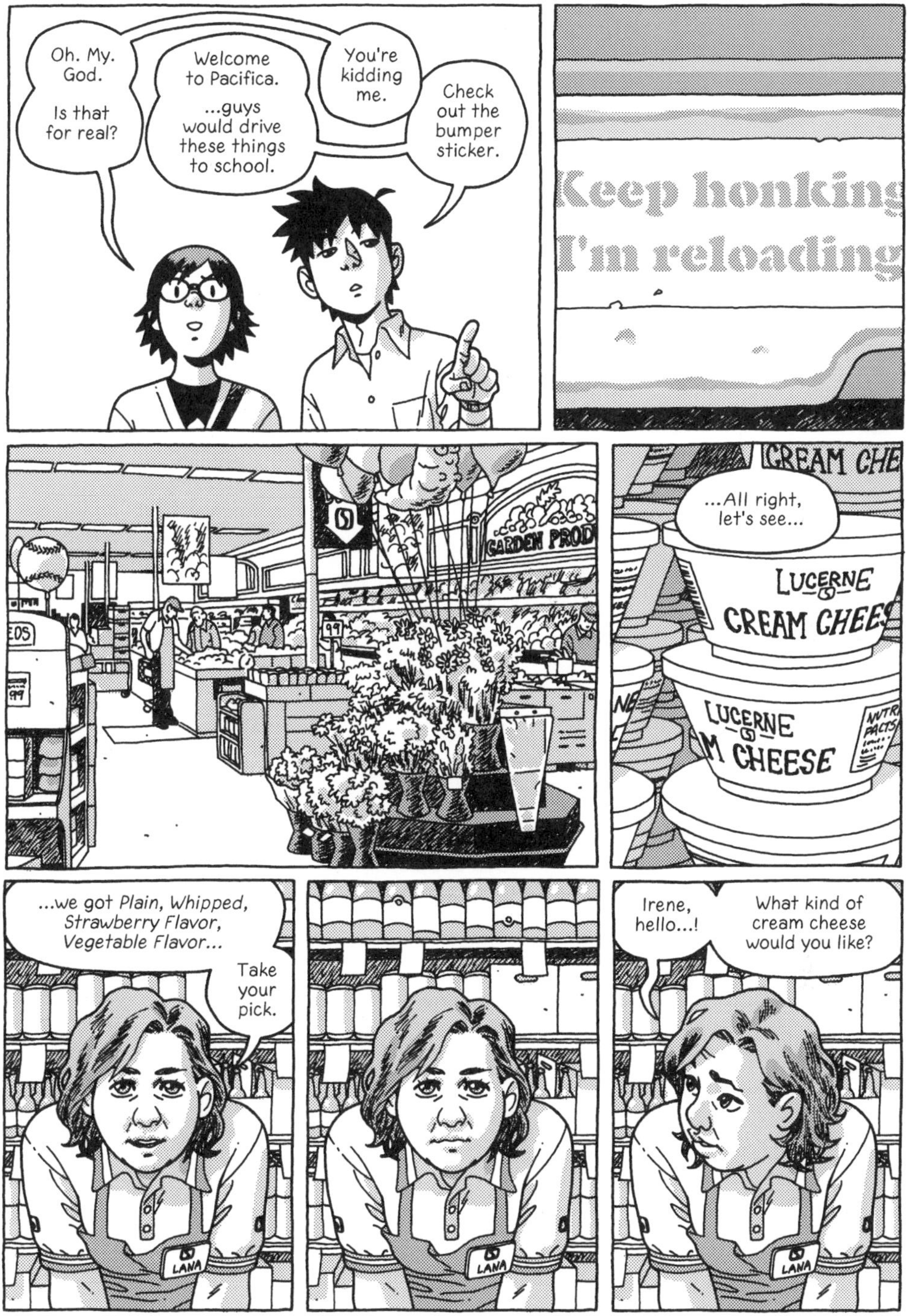
Oh. My. God.
Is that for real?
Welcome to Pacifica.
...guys would drive these things to school.
You're kidding me.
Check out the bumper sticker.
Keep honking I'm reloading
GARDEN PROD
CREAM CHE
...All right, let's see...
LUCERNE
CREAM CHEES
LUCERNE
M CHEESE
...we got *Plain, Whipped, Strawberry Flavor, Vegetable Flavor...*
Take your pick.
LANA
LANA
Irene, hello...!
What kind of cream cheese would you like?
LANA

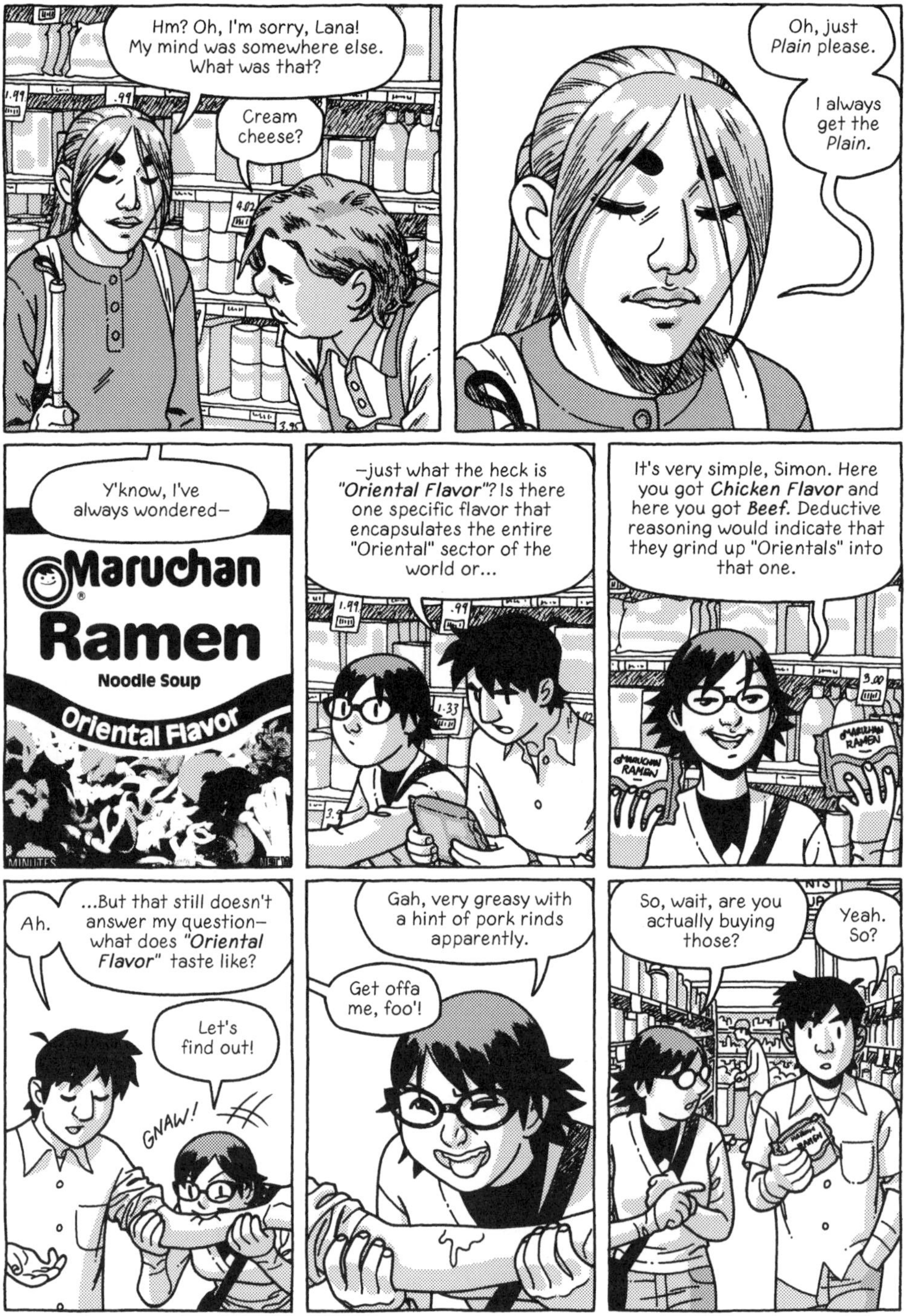
Hm? Oh, I'm sorry, Lana! My mind was somewhere else. What was that?
Cream cheese?
Oh, just *Plain* please.
I always get the *Plain.*
Y'know, I've always wondered–
Maruchan Ramen Noodle Soup Oriental Flavor
–just what the heck is *"Oriental Flavor"*? Is there one specific flavor that encapsulates the entire "Oriental" sector of the world or...
It's very simple, Simon. Here you got ***Chicken Flavor*** and here you got ***Beef.*** Deductive reasoning would indicate that they grind up "Orientals" into that one.
Ah.
...But that still doesn't answer my question– what does *"Oriental Flavor"* taste like?
Let's find out!
GNAW!
Gah, very greasy with a hint of pork rinds apparently.
Get offa me, foo'!
So, wait, are you actually buying those?
Yeah. So?

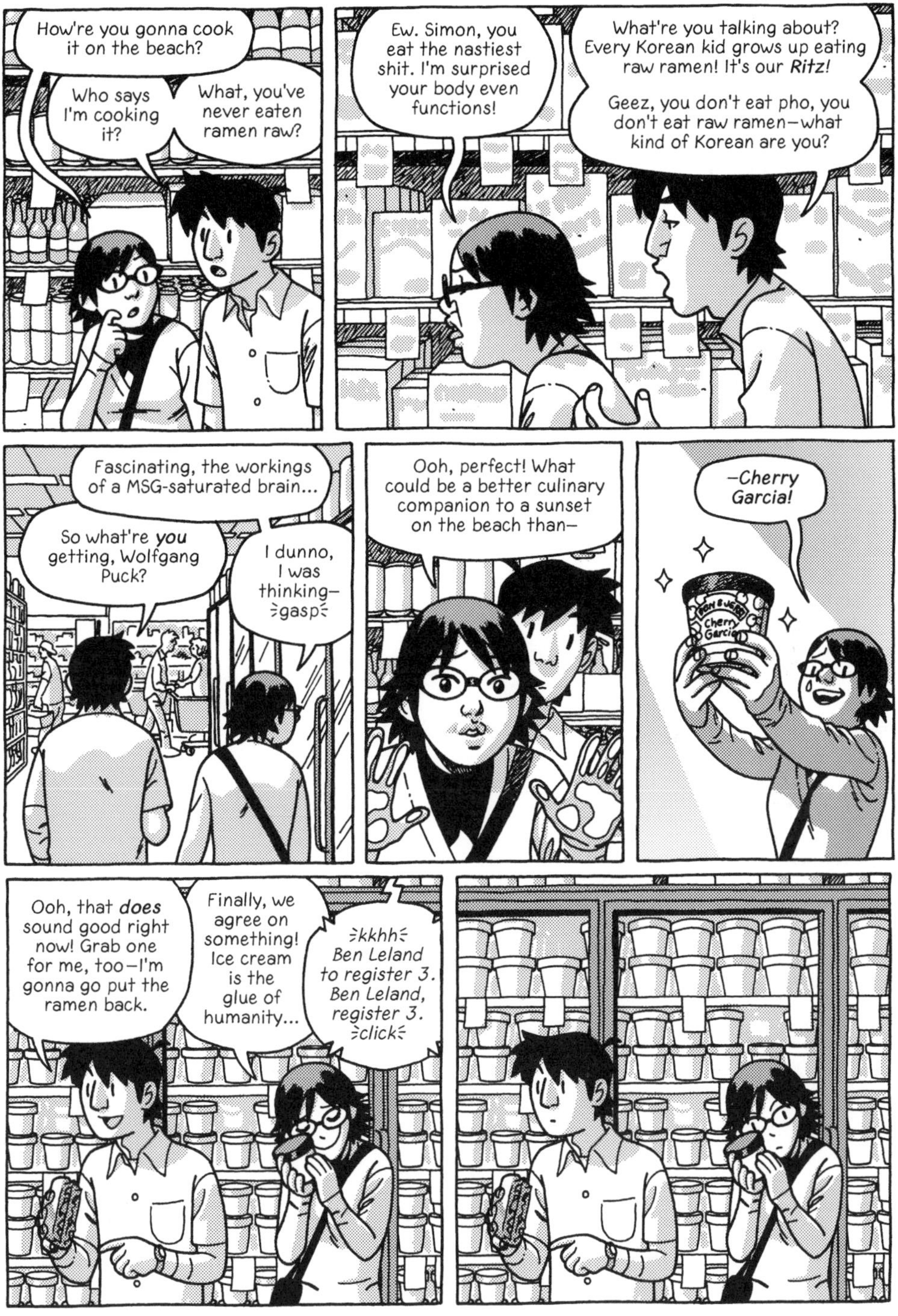
How're you gonna cook it on the beach?
Who says I'm cooking it?
What, you've never eaten ramen raw?
Ew. Simon, you eat the nastiest shit. I'm surprised your body even functions!
What're you talking about? Every Korean kid grows up eating raw ramen! It's our *Ritz!*
Geez, you don't eat pho, you don't eat raw ramen—what kind of Korean are you?
Fascinating, the workings of a MSG-saturated brain...
So what're *you* getting, Wolfgang Puck?
I dunno, I was thinking— ⁼gasp⁼
Ooh, perfect! What could be a better culinary companion to a sunset on the beach than—
—*Cherry Garcia!*
Ben & Jerry's
Cherry Garcia
Ooh, that *does* sound good right now! Grab one for me, too—I'm gonna go put the ramen back.
Finally, we agree on something! Ice cream is the glue of humanity...
⁼*kkhh*⁼ *Ben Leland to register 3. Ben Leland, register 3.* ⁼*click*⁼

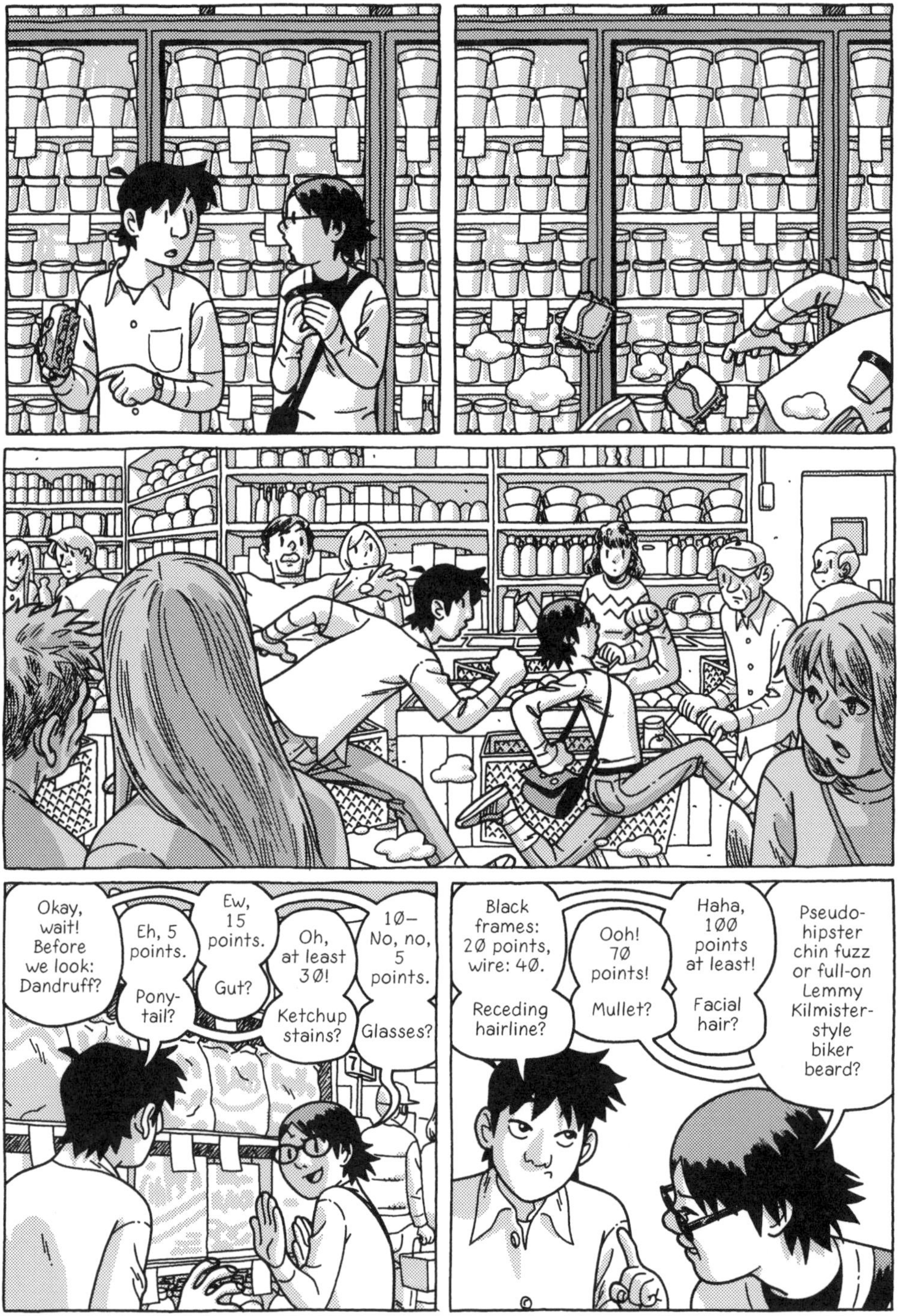
Okay, wait! Before we look: Dandruff?
Eh, 5 points.
Pony-tail?
Ew, 15 points.
Gut?
Oh, at least 3Ø!
Ketchup stains?
1Ø— No, no, 5 points.
Glasses?
Black frames: 2Ø points, wire: 4Ø.
Receding hairline?
Ooh! 7Ø points!
Mullet?
Haha, 1ØØ points at least!
Facial hair?
Pseudo-hipster chin fuzz or full-on Lemmy Kilmister-style biker beard?

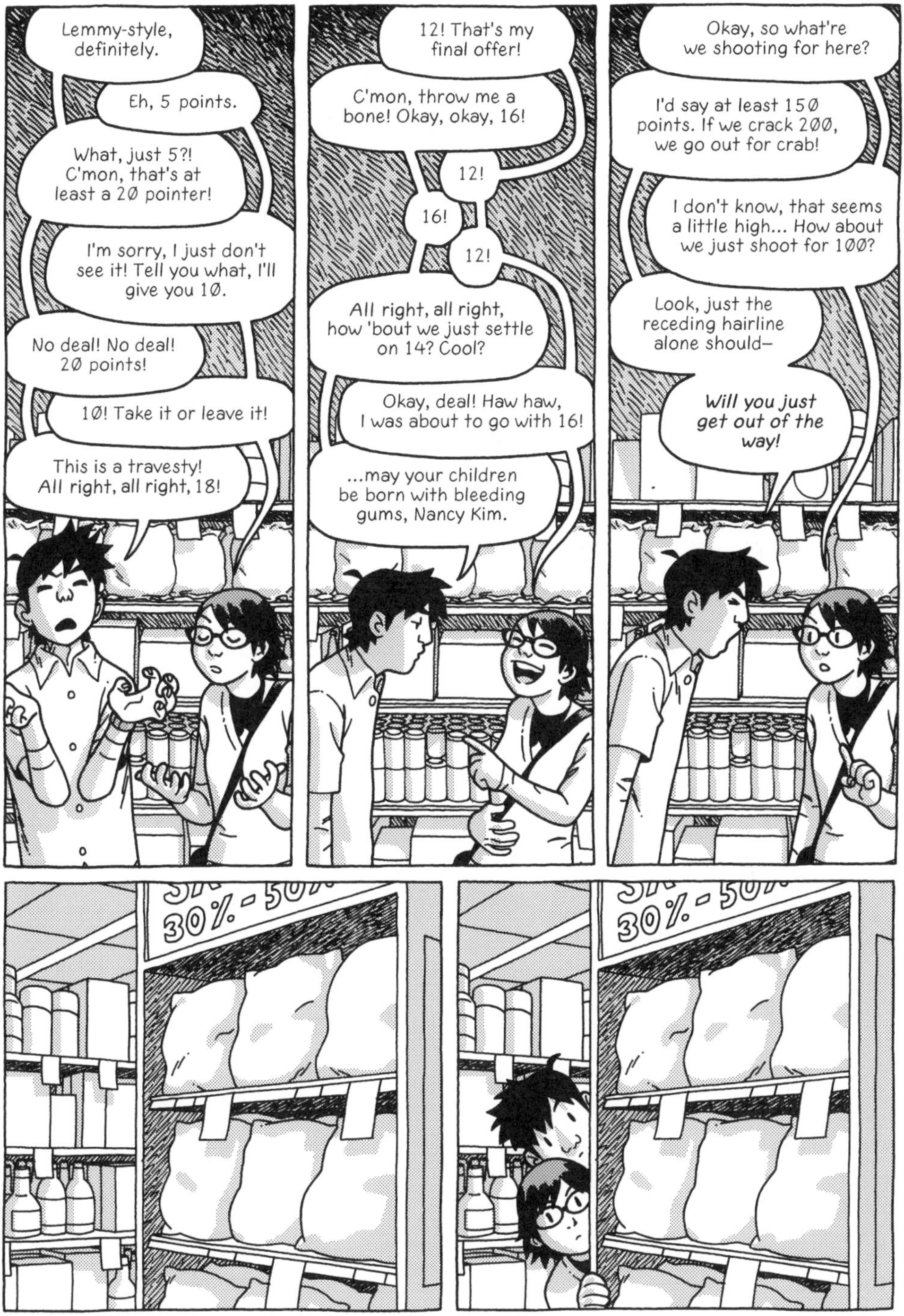

Lemmy-style, definitely.
Eh, 5 points.
What, just 5?! C'mon, that's at least a 2Ø pointer!
I'm sorry, I just don't see it! Tell you what, I'll give you 1Ø.
No deal! No deal! 2Ø points!
1Ø! Take it or leave it!
This is a travesty! All right, all right, 18!
12! That's my final offer!
C'mon, throw me a bone! Okay, okay, 16!
12!
16!
12!
All right, all right, how 'bout we just settle on 14? Cool?
Okay, deal! Haw haw, I was about to go with 16!
...may your children be born with bleeding gums, Nancy Kim.
Okay, so what're we shooting for here?
I'd say at least 15Ø points. If we crack 2ØØ, we go out for crab!
I don't know, that seems a little high... How about we just shoot for 1ØØ?
Look, just the receding hairline alone should–
Will you just get out of the way!
30% - 50%
30% - 50%

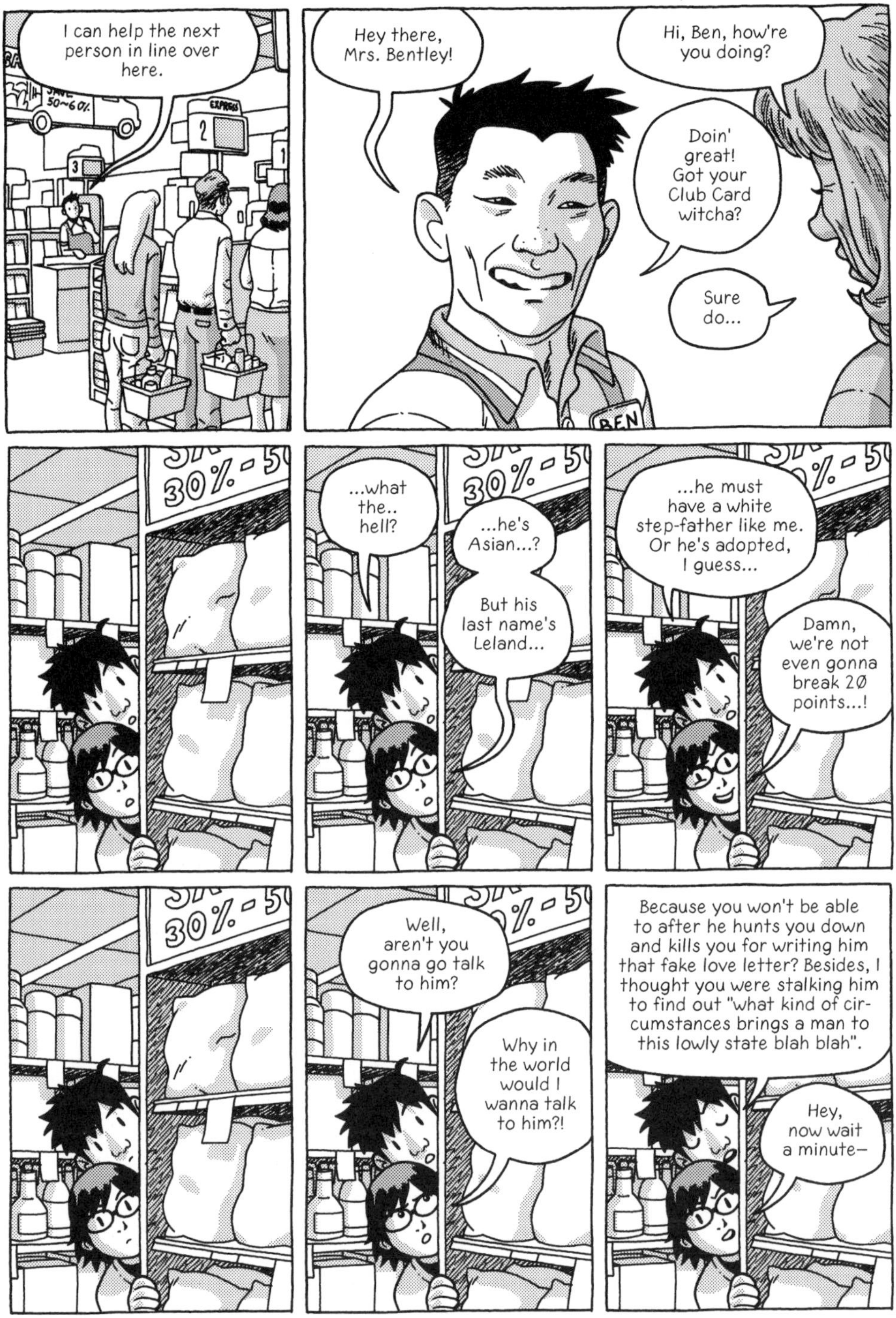
I can help the next person in line over here.
SAVE 50~60%
EXPRESS
3
2
1
Hey there, Mrs. Bentley!
Hi, Ben, how're you doing?
Doin' great! Got your Club Card witcha?
Sure do...
BEN
30%-5
...what the.. hell?
...he's Asian...?
But his last name's Leland...
...he must have a white step-father like me. Or he's adopted, I guess...
Damn, we're not even gonna break 2Ø points...!
Well, aren't you gonna go talk to him?
Why in the world would I wanna talk to him?!
Because you won't be able to after he hunts you down and kills you for writing him that fake love letter? Besides, I thought you were stalking him to find out "what kind of circumstances brings a man to this lowly state blah blah".
Hey, now wait a minute—

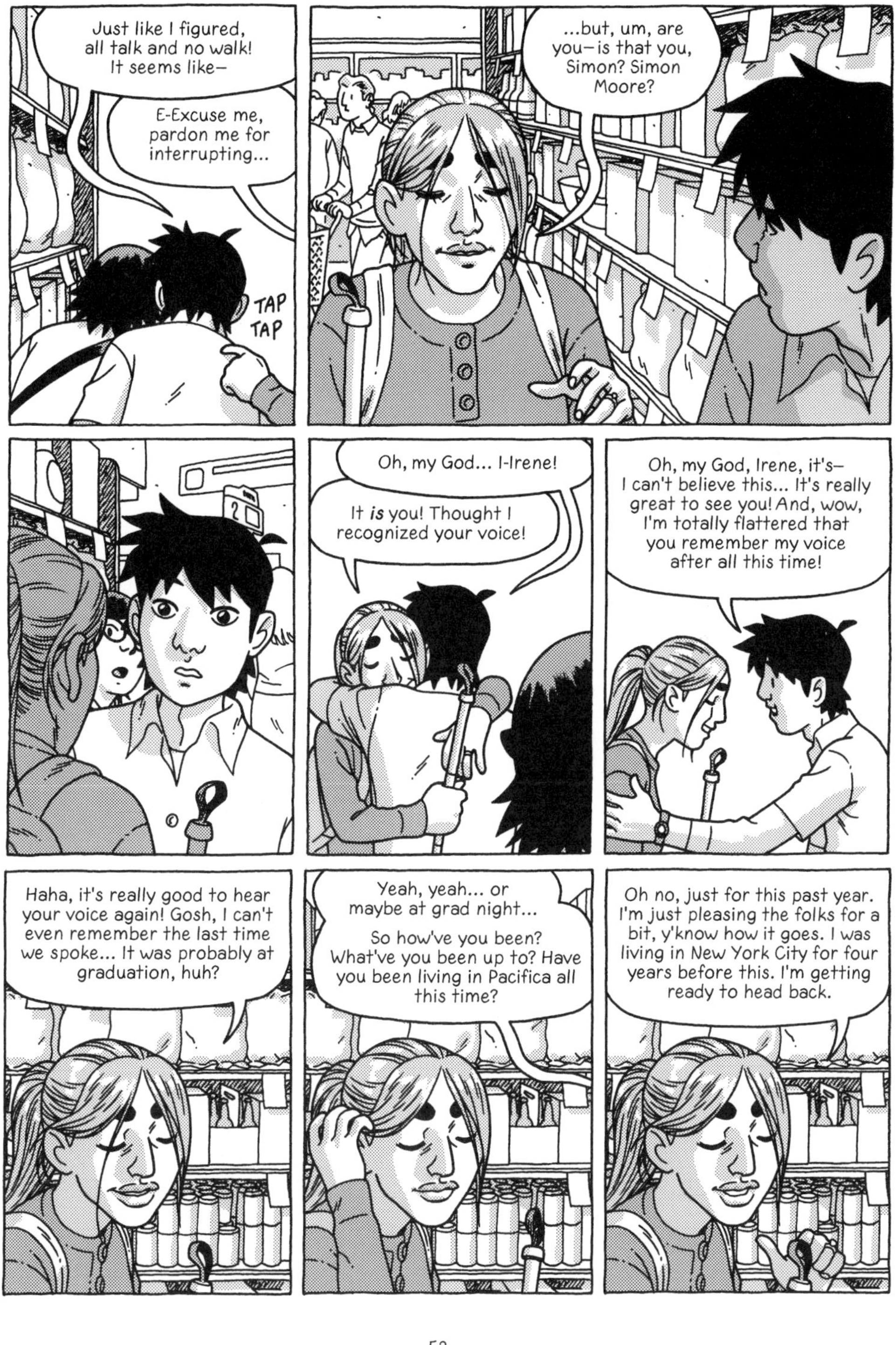
Just like I figured, all talk and no walk! It seems like–
E-Excuse me, pardon me for interrupting...
TAP TAP
...but, um, are you– is that you, Simon? Simon Moore?
Oh, my God... I-Irene!
It *is* you! Thought I recognized your voice!
Oh, my God, Irene, it's– I can't believe this... It's really great to see you! And, wow, I'm totally flattered that you remember my voice after all this time!
Haha, it's really good to hear your voice again! Gosh, I can't even remember the last time we spoke... It was probably at graduation, huh?
Yeah, yeah... or maybe at grad night...
So how've you been? What've you been up to? Have you been living in Pacifica all this time?
Oh no, just for this past year. I'm just pleasing the folks for a bit, y'know how it goes. I was living in New York City for four years before this. I'm getting ready to head back.

Wow, New York, huh? That's great!

How about you?

Never left the Bay Area myself. Just dragged my skinny butt to Oakland.

Really? Actually I was just there yesterday visiting a friend!

Oh, I— Shoot! I wish I'd known, we coulda gotten together for lunch or something.

Yeah, like maybe at a *pho restaurant*, for example.

야! 닥쳐!*

Hey, who's that there with you, Simon?

Irene, there you are! I got the eggs—that should be everything.

Oh, okay, great! Thanks, Lana.

Geez, I wish I'd run into you a little sooner, Simon. Someone's coming to pick me up any minute now—I should go wait outside...

Oh okay, that's cool, I don't wanna get in your way here.

Listen, it was really great to see you though! Why don't— Let's get together sometime and, uh, catch up and stuff.

Yeah yeah, sure. Why don't I give you my parents' number and—

Oh, I still got it in my little wallet address book somewhere. Still have the same one from high school. Heh heh...

Oh, ha ha... Well... I'll talk to you soon then. Take it easy, Simon.

Yeah, you too. See ya!

* "Hey! Shaddup!" in Korean

54

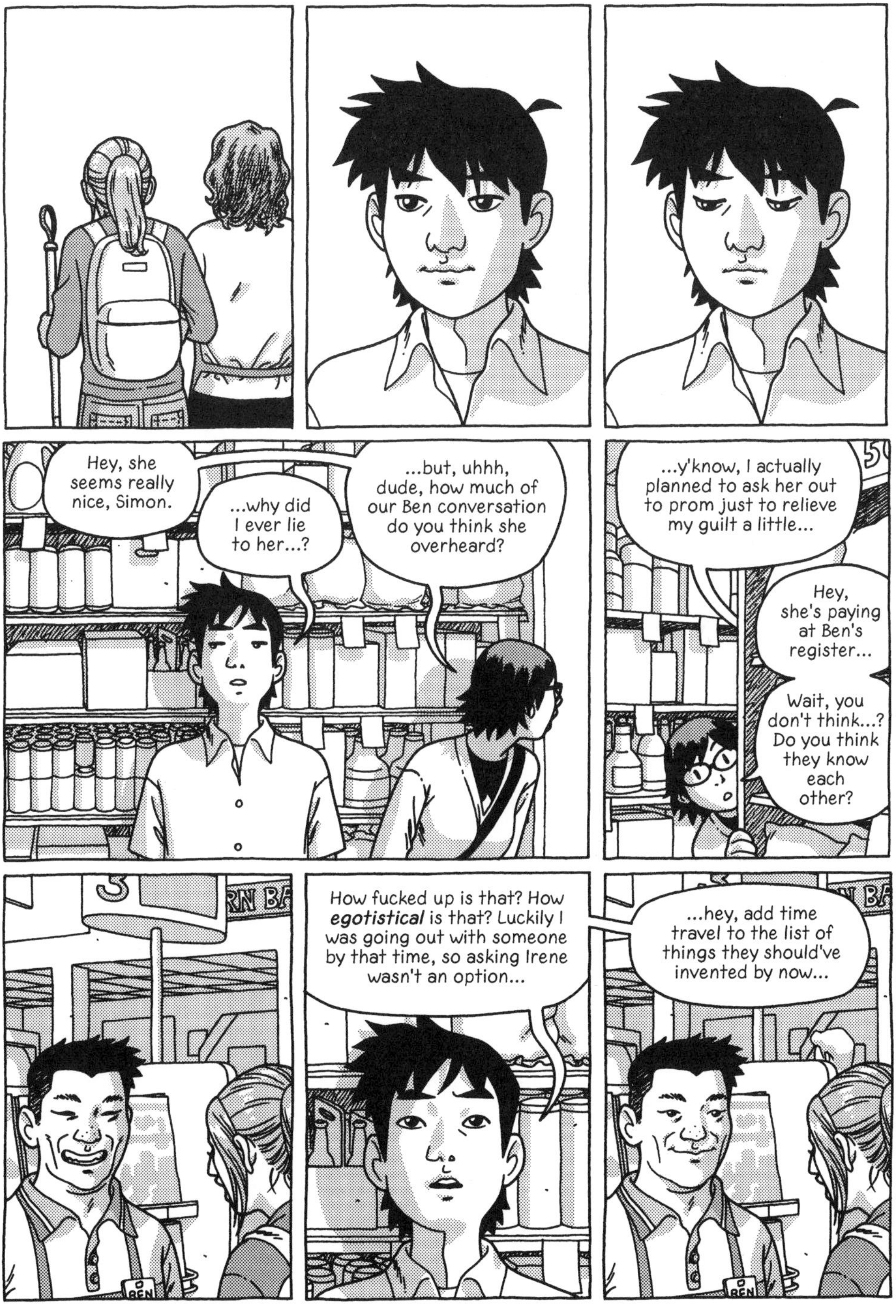
Hey, she seems really nice, Simon.
...why did I ever lie to her...?
...but, uhhh, dude, how much of our Ben conversation do you think she overheard?
...y'know, I actually planned to ask her out to prom just to relieve my guilt a little...
Hey, she's paying at Ben's register...
Wait, you don't think...? Do you think they know each other?
How fucked up is that? How *egotistical* is that? Luckily I was going out with someone by that time, so asking Irene wasn't an option...
...hey, add time travel to the list of things they should've invented by now...
BEN
BEN

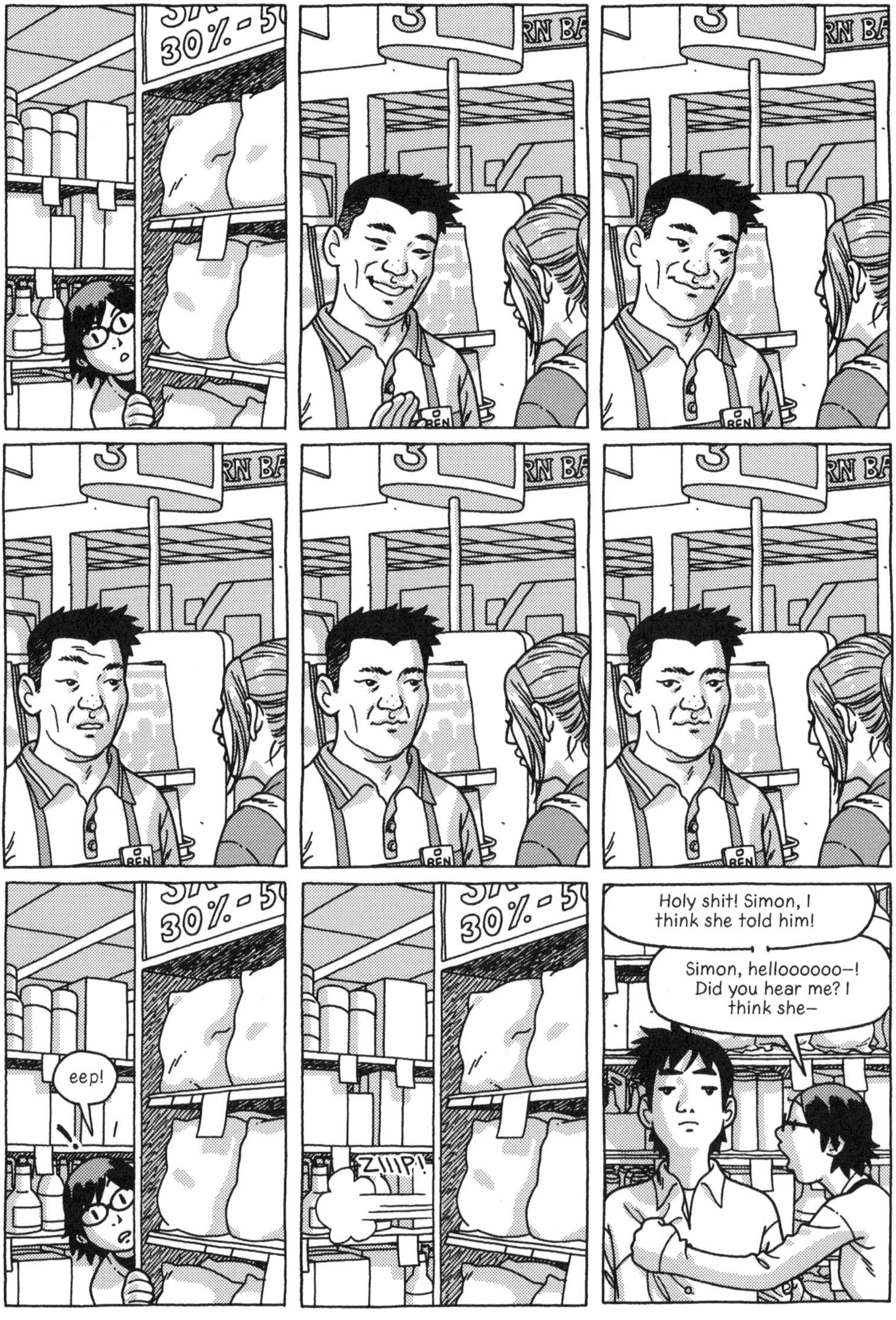
30% - 5
BEN
eep!
ZIIIP!
Holy shit! Simon, I think she told him!
Simon, helloooooo—! Did you hear me? I think she—

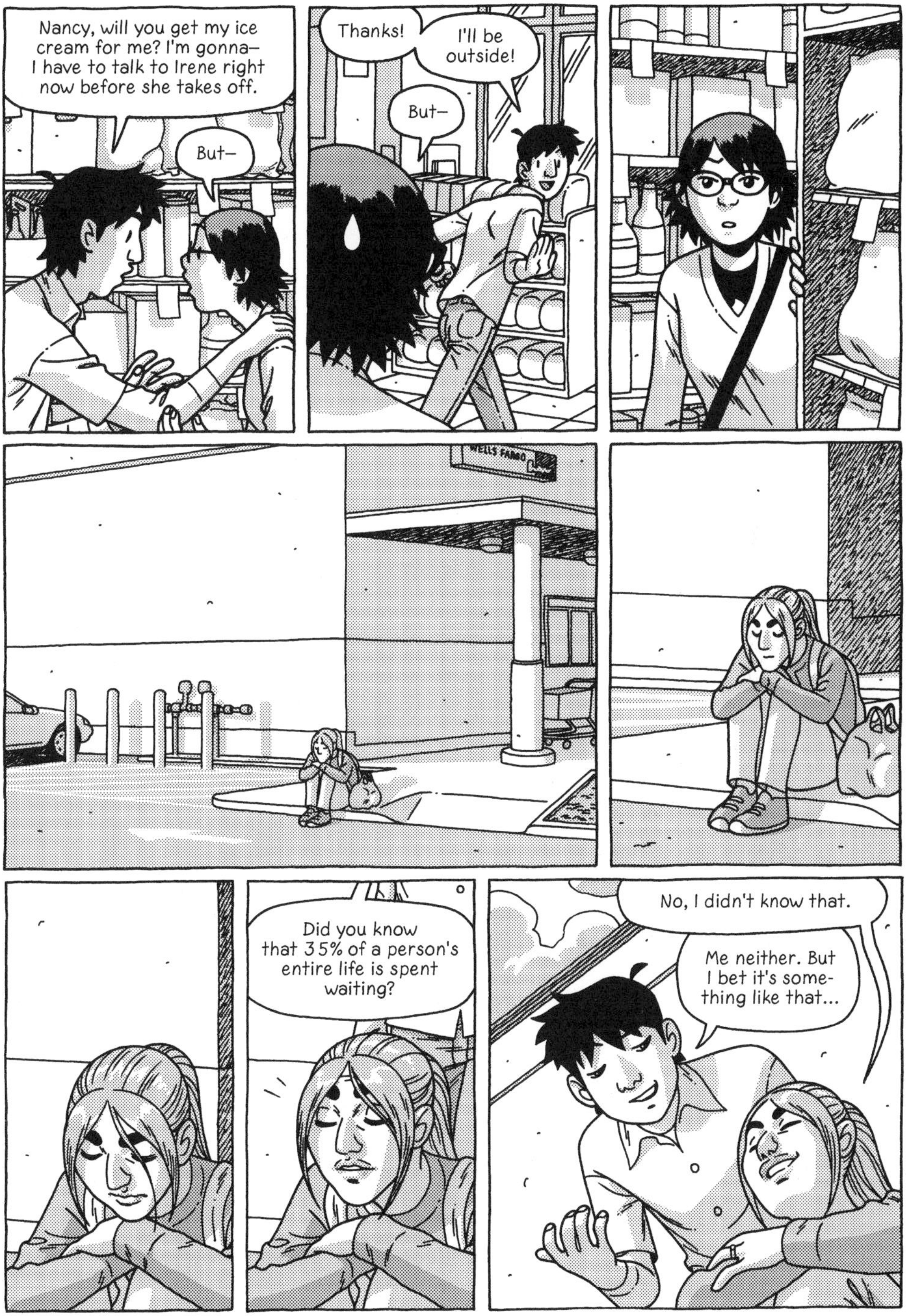

Nancy, will you get my ice cream for me? I'm gonna– I have to talk to Irene right now before she takes off.
But–
Thanks!
I'll be outside!
But–
WELLS FARGO
Did you know that 35% of a person's entire life is spent waiting?
No, I didn't know that.
Me neither. But I bet it's something like that...

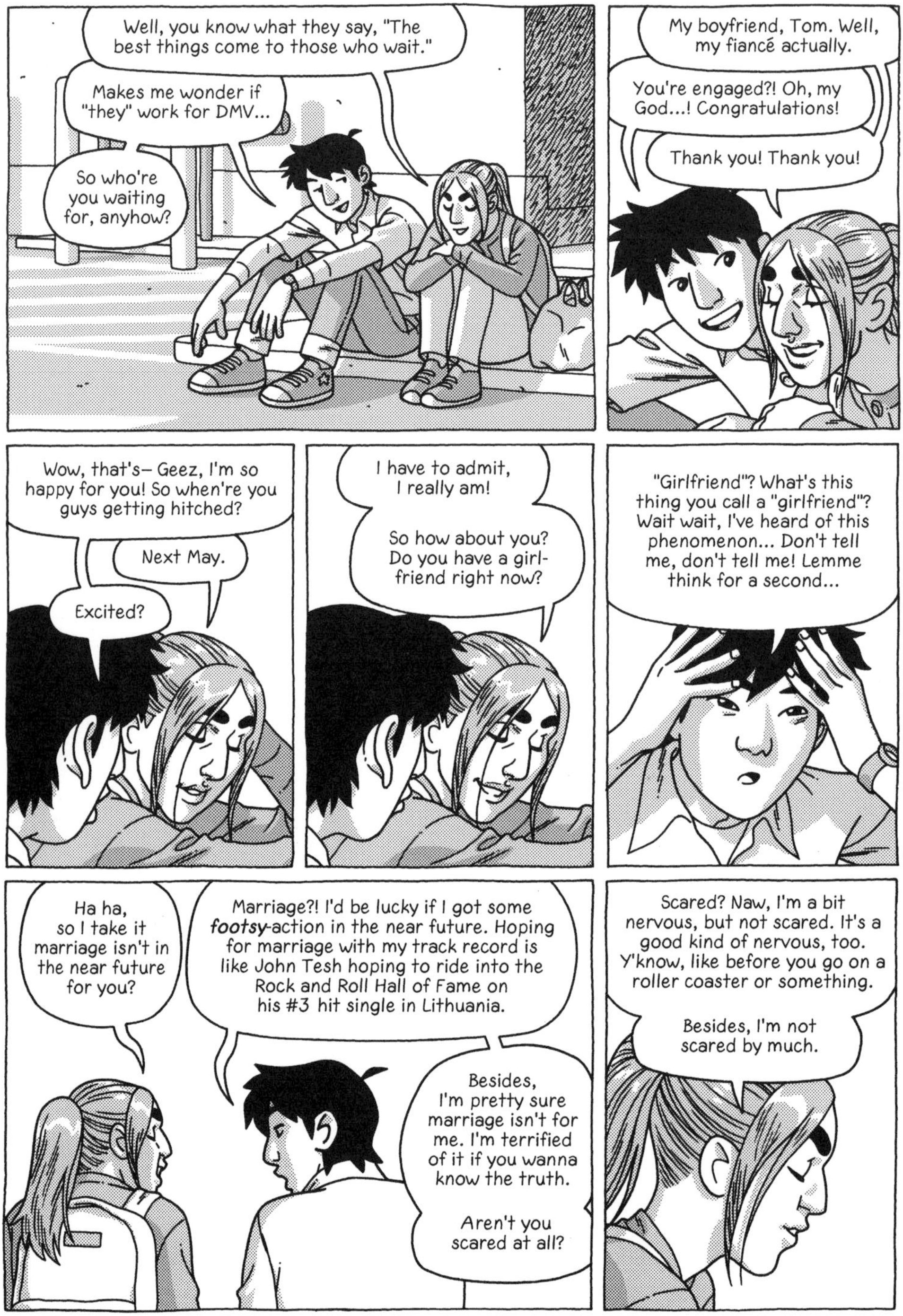

Well, you know what they say, "The best things come to those who wait."
Makes me wonder if "they" work for DMV...
So who're you waiting for, anyhow?
My boyfriend, Tom. Well, my fiancé actually.
You're engaged?! Oh, my God...! Congratulations!
Thank you! Thank you!
Wow, that's– Geez, I'm so happy for you! So when're you guys getting hitched?
Next May.
Excited?
I have to admit, I really am!
So how about you? Do you have a girl-friend right now?
"Girlfriend"? What's this thing you call a "girlfriend"? Wait wait, I've heard of this phenomenon... Don't tell me, don't tell me! Lemme think for a second...
Ha ha, so I take it marriage isn't in the near future for you?
Marriage?! I'd be lucky if I got some *footsy*-action in the near future. Hoping for marriage with my track record is like John Tesh hoping to ride into the Rock and Roll Hall of Fame on his #3 hit single in Lithuania.
Besides, I'm pretty sure marriage isn't for me. I'm terrified of it if you wanna know the truth.
Aren't you scared at all?
Scared? Naw, I'm a bit nervous, but not scared. It's a good kind of nervous, too. Y'know, like before you go on a roller coaster or something.
Besides, I'm not scared by much.

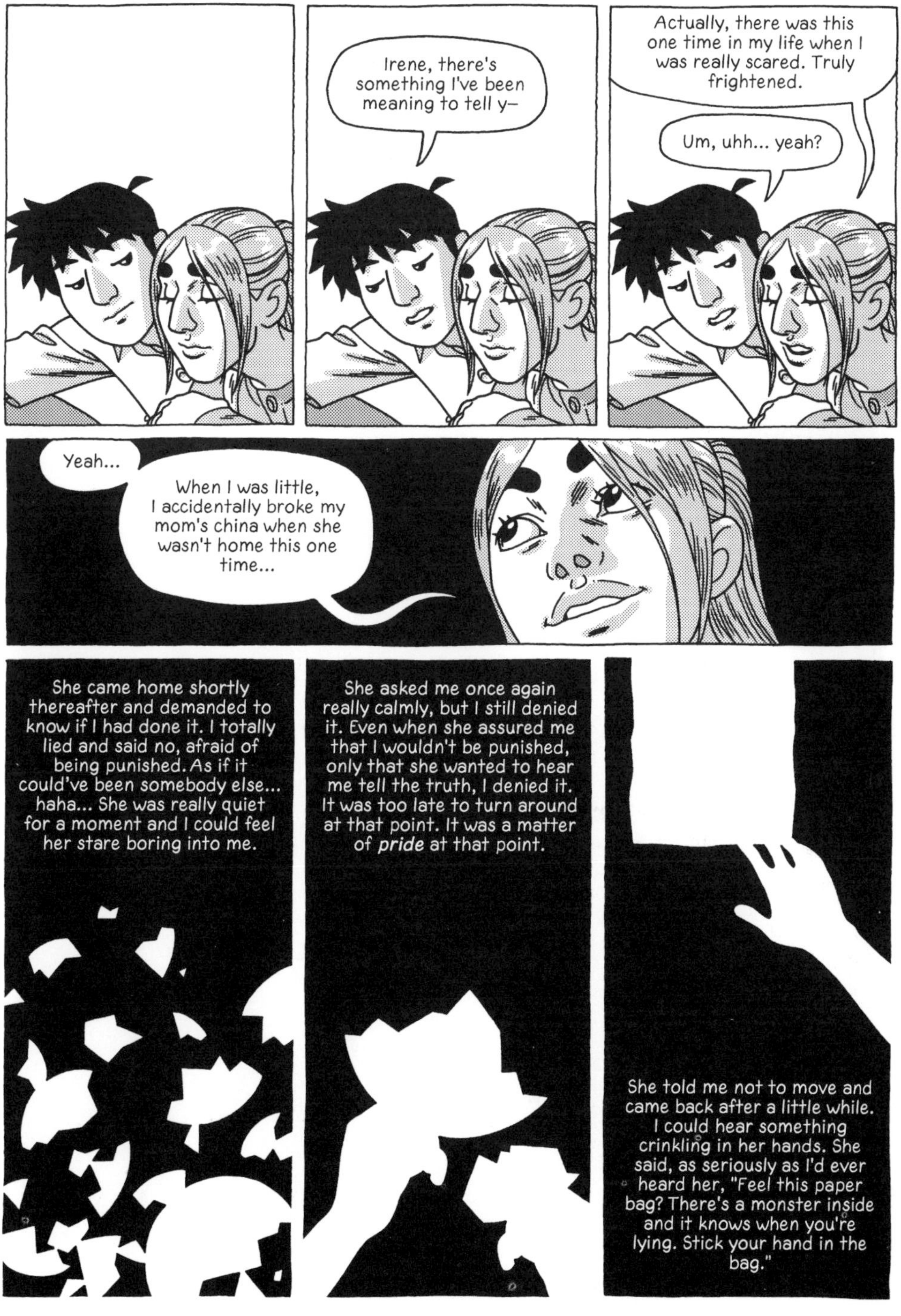
Irene, there's something I've been meaning to tell y–
Actually, there was this one time in my life when I was really scared. Truly frightened.
Um, uhh... yeah?
Yeah...
When I was little, I accidentally broke my mom's china when she wasn't home this one time...
She came home shortly thereafter and demanded to know if I had done it. I totally lied and said no, afraid of being punished. As if it could've been somebody else... haha... She was really quiet for a moment and I could feel her stare boring into me.
She asked me once again really calmly, but I still denied it. Even when she assured me that I wouldn't be punished, only that she wanted to hear me tell the truth, I denied it. It was too late to turn around at that point. It was a matter of *pride* at that point.
She told me not to move and came back after a little while. I could hear something crinkling in her hands. She said, as seriously as I'd ever heard her, "Feel this paper bag? There's a monster inside and it knows when you're lying. Stick your hand in the bag."

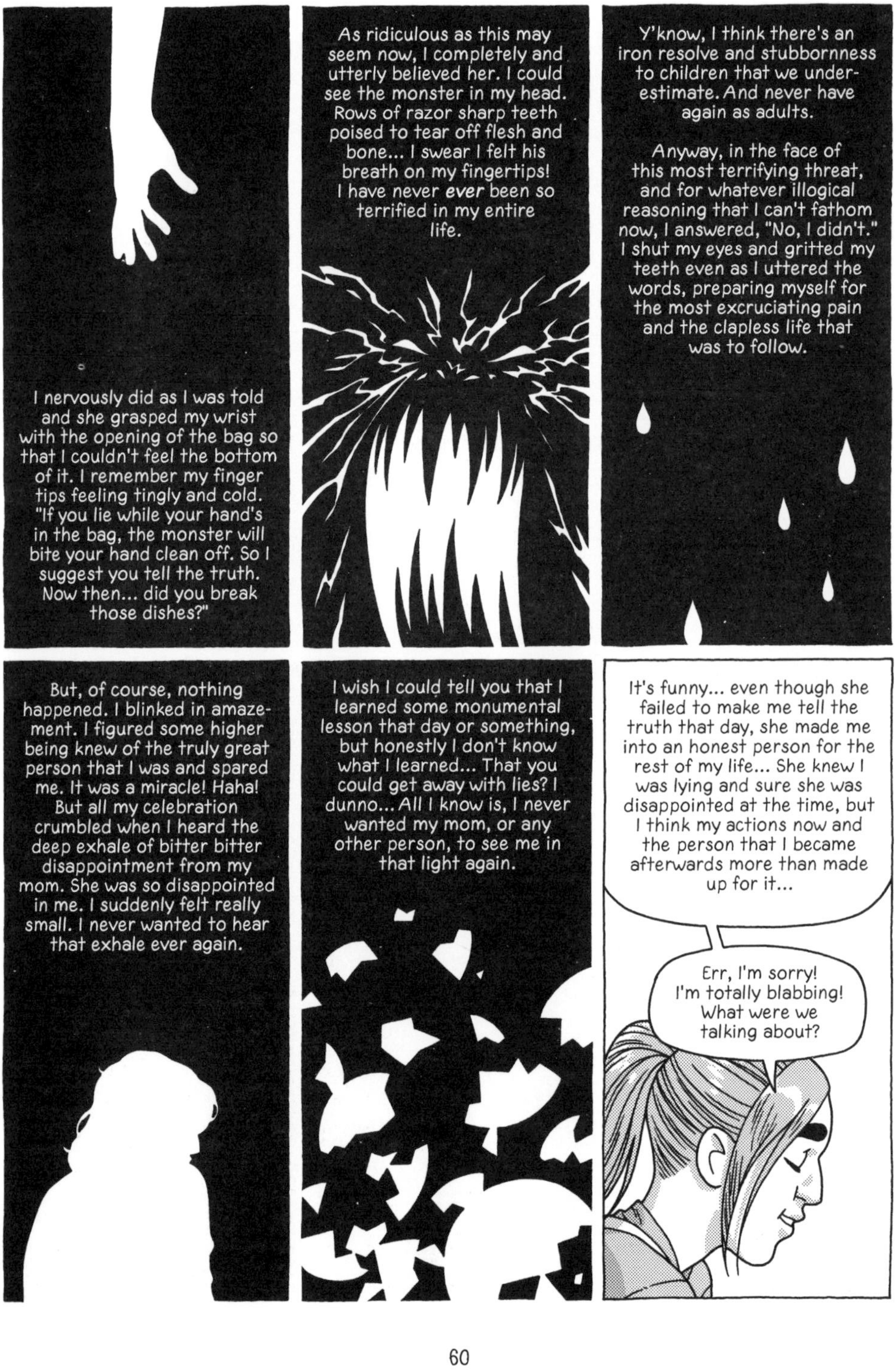
I nervously did as I was told and she grasped my wrist with the opening of the bag so that I couldn't feel the bottom of it. I remember my finger tips feeling tingly and cold. "If you lie while your hand's in the bag, the monster will bite your hand clean off. So I suggest you tell the truth. Now then... did you break those dishes?"
As ridiculous as this may seem now, I completely and utterly believed her. I could see the monster in my head. Rows of razor sharp teeth poised to tear off flesh and bone... I swear I felt his breath on my fingertips! I have never *ever* been so terrified in my entire life.
Y'know, I think there's an iron resolve and stubbornness to children that we underestimate. And never have again as adults.
Anyway, in the face of this most terrifying threat, and for whatever illogical reasoning that I can't fathom now, I answered, "No, I didn't." I shut my eyes and gritted my teeth even as I uttered the words, preparing myself for the most excruciating pain and the clapless life that was to follow.
But, of course, nothing happened. I blinked in amazement. I figured some higher being knew of the truly great person that I was and spared me. It was a miracle! Haha! But all my celebration crumbled when I heard the deep exhale of bitter bitter disappointment from my mom. She was so disappointed in me. I suddenly felt really small. I never wanted to hear that exhale ever again.
I wish I could tell you that I learned some monumental lesson that day or something, but honestly I don't know what I learned... That you could get away with lies? I dunno... All I know is, I never wanted my mom, or any other person, to see me in that light again.
It's funny... even though she failed to make me tell the truth that day, she made me into an honest person for the rest of my life... She knew I was lying and sure she was disappointed at the time, but I think my actions now and the person that I became afterwards more than made up for it...
Err, I'm sorry! I'm totally blabbing! What were we talking about?

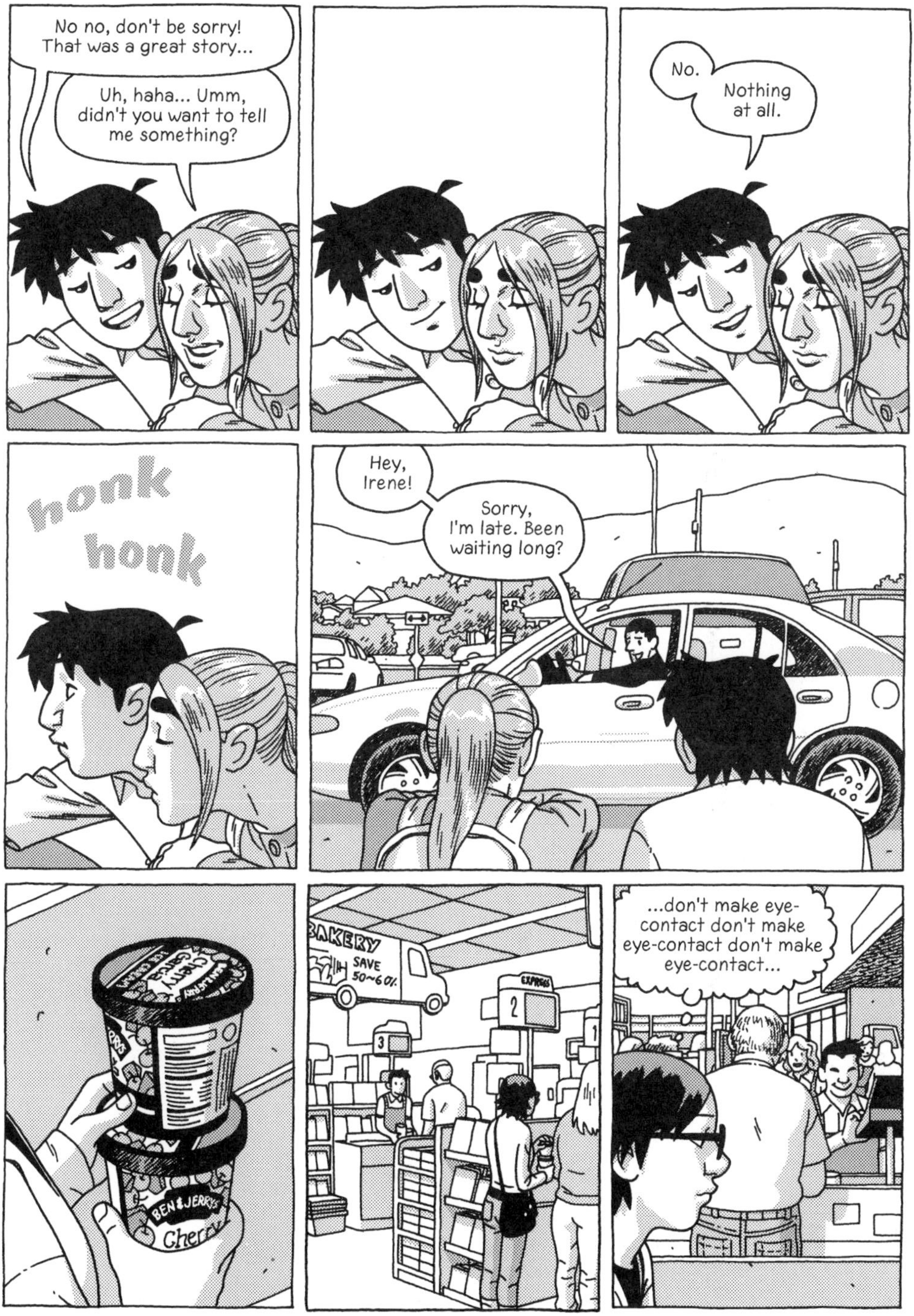
No no, don't be sorry! That was a great story...
Uh, haha... Umm, didn't you want to tell me something?
No.
Nothing at all.
honk
honk
Hey, Irene!
Sorry, I'm late. Been waiting long?
Cherry Garcia
Cherry
BAKERY
SAVE 50~60%
EXPRESS
...don't make eye-contact don't make eye-contact don't make eye-contact...

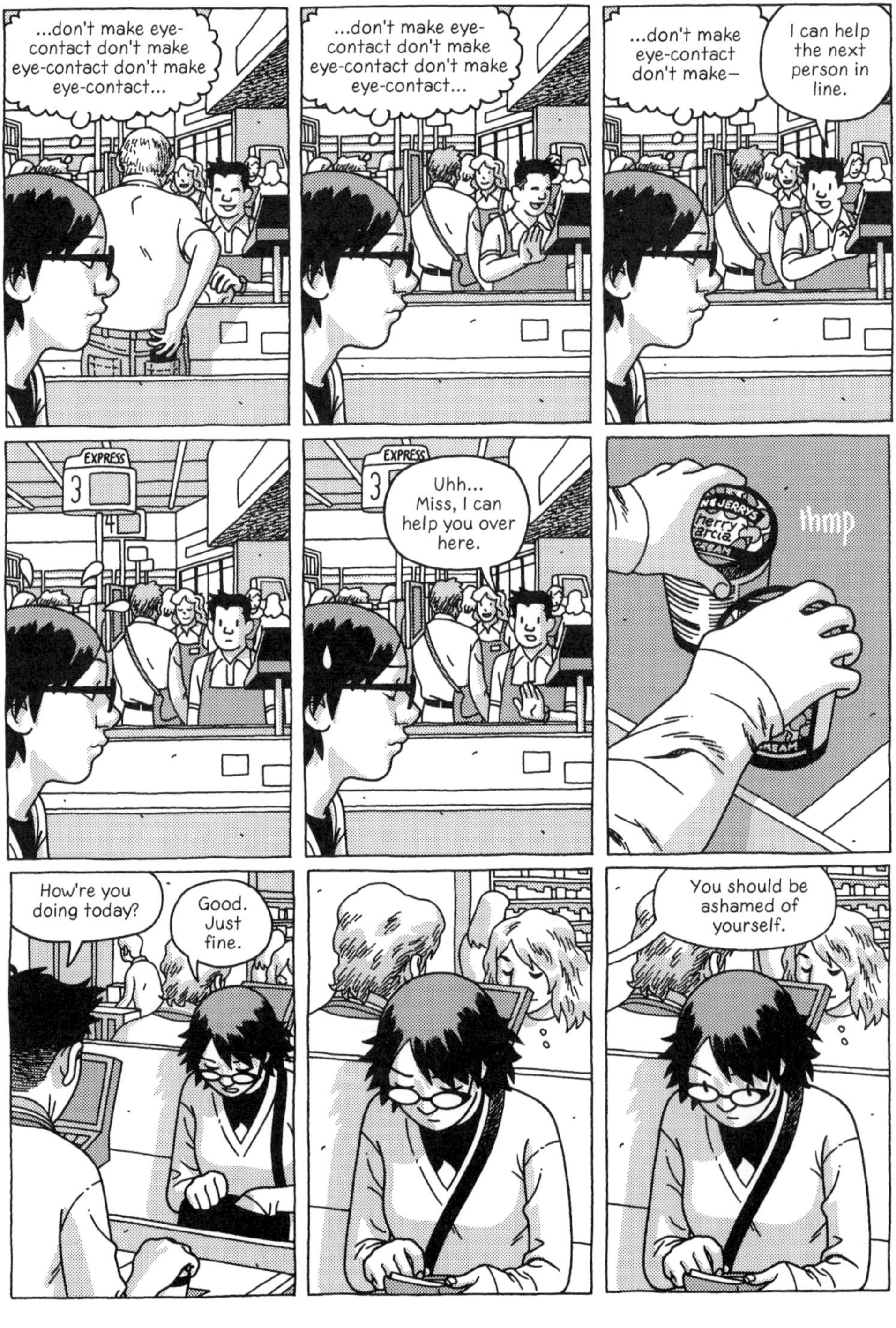

...don't make eye-contact don't make eye-contact don't make eye-contact...
...don't make eye-contact don't make eye-contact don't make eye-contact...
...don't make eye-contact don't make–
I can help the next person in line.
EXPRESS
3
4
EXPRESS
3
Uhh... Miss, I can help you over here.
thmp
How're you doing today?
Good. Just fine.
You should be ashamed of yourself.

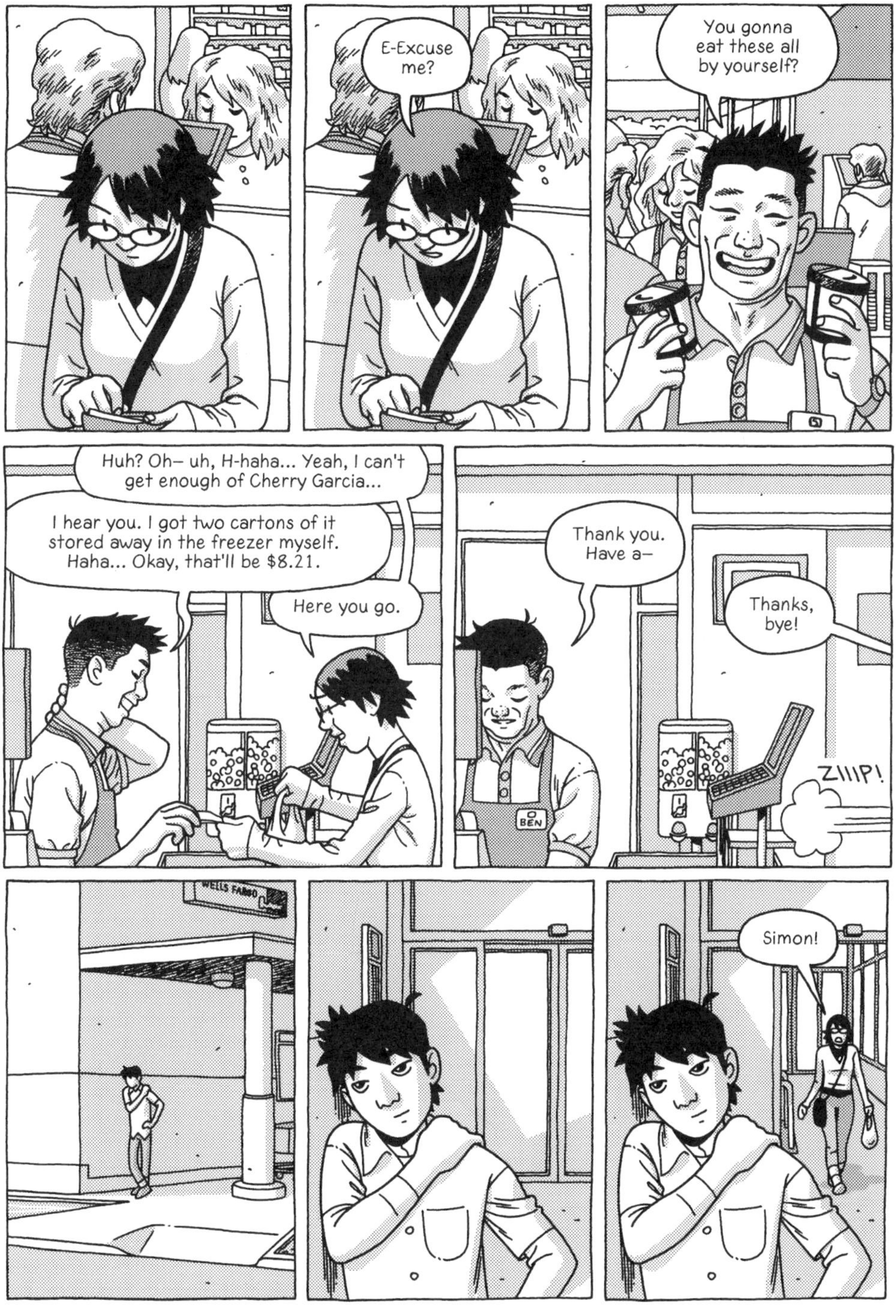
E-Excuse me?
You gonna eat these all by yourself?
Huh? Oh– uh, H-haha... Yeah, I can't get enough of Cherry Garcia...
I hear you. I got two cartons of it stored away in the freezer myself. Haha... Okay, that'll be $8.21.
Here you go.
Thank you. Have a–
Thanks, bye!
BEN
ZIIIP!
WELLS FARGO
Simon!

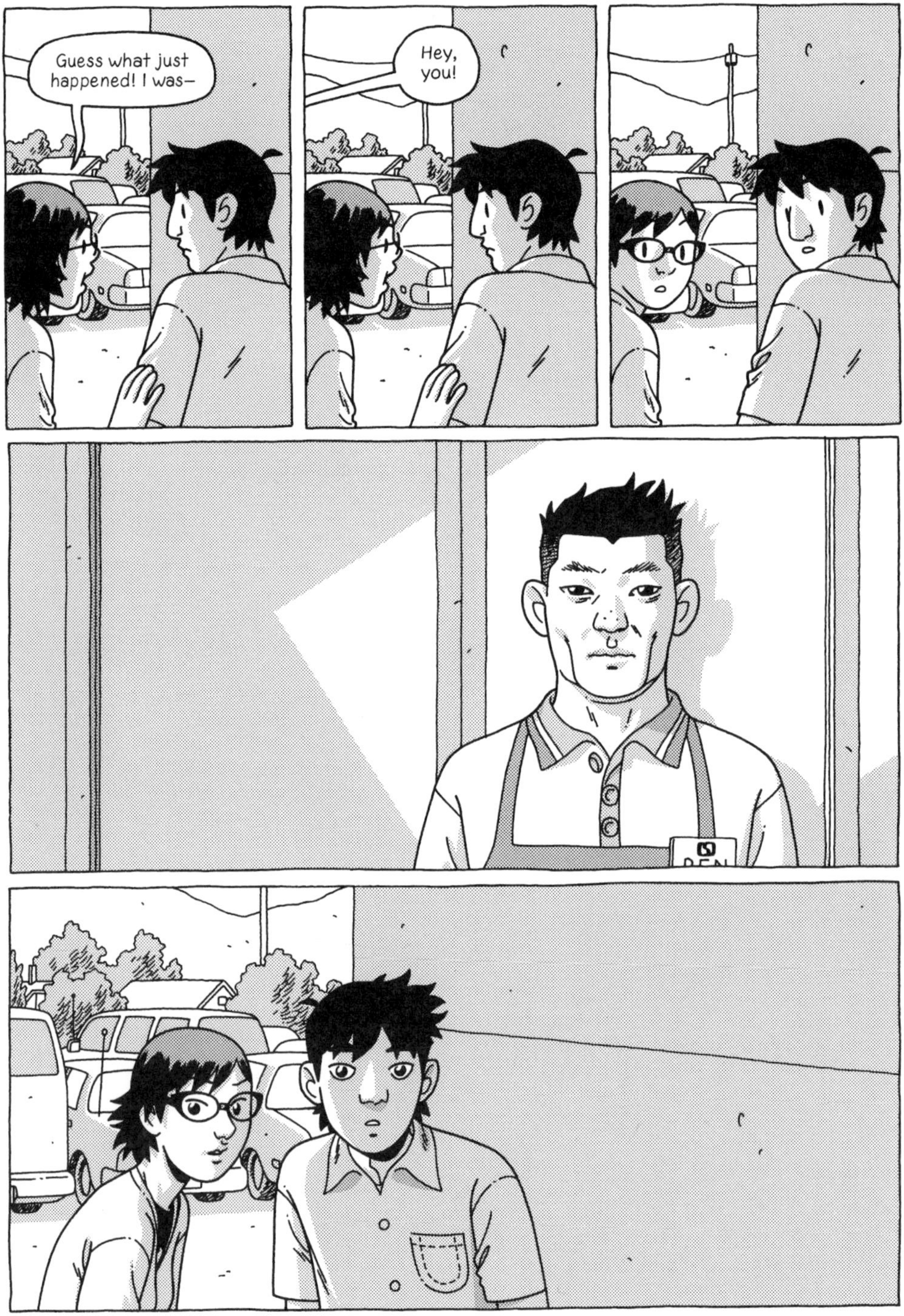
Guess what just happened! I was—
Hey, you!

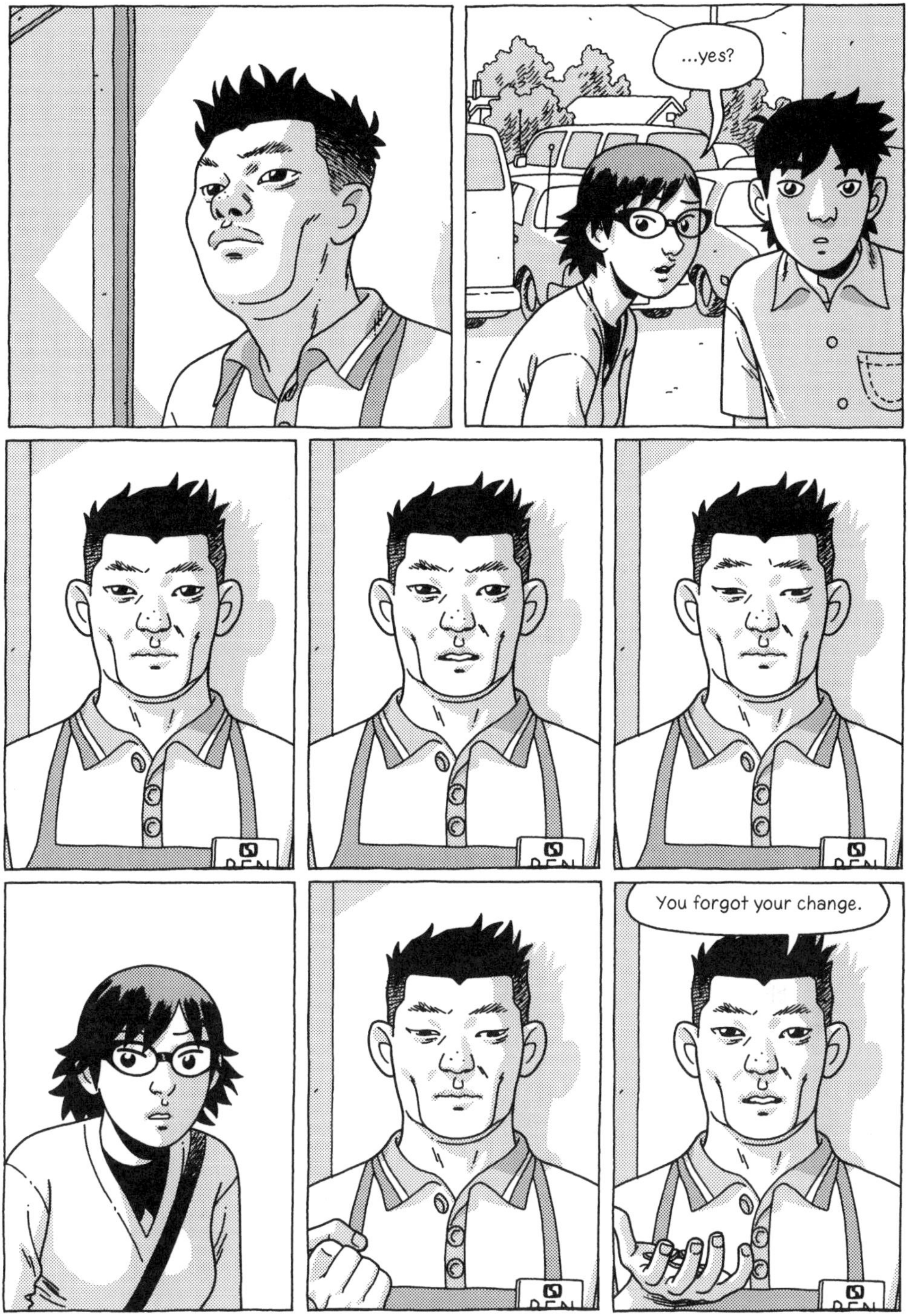
...yes?
You forgot your change.

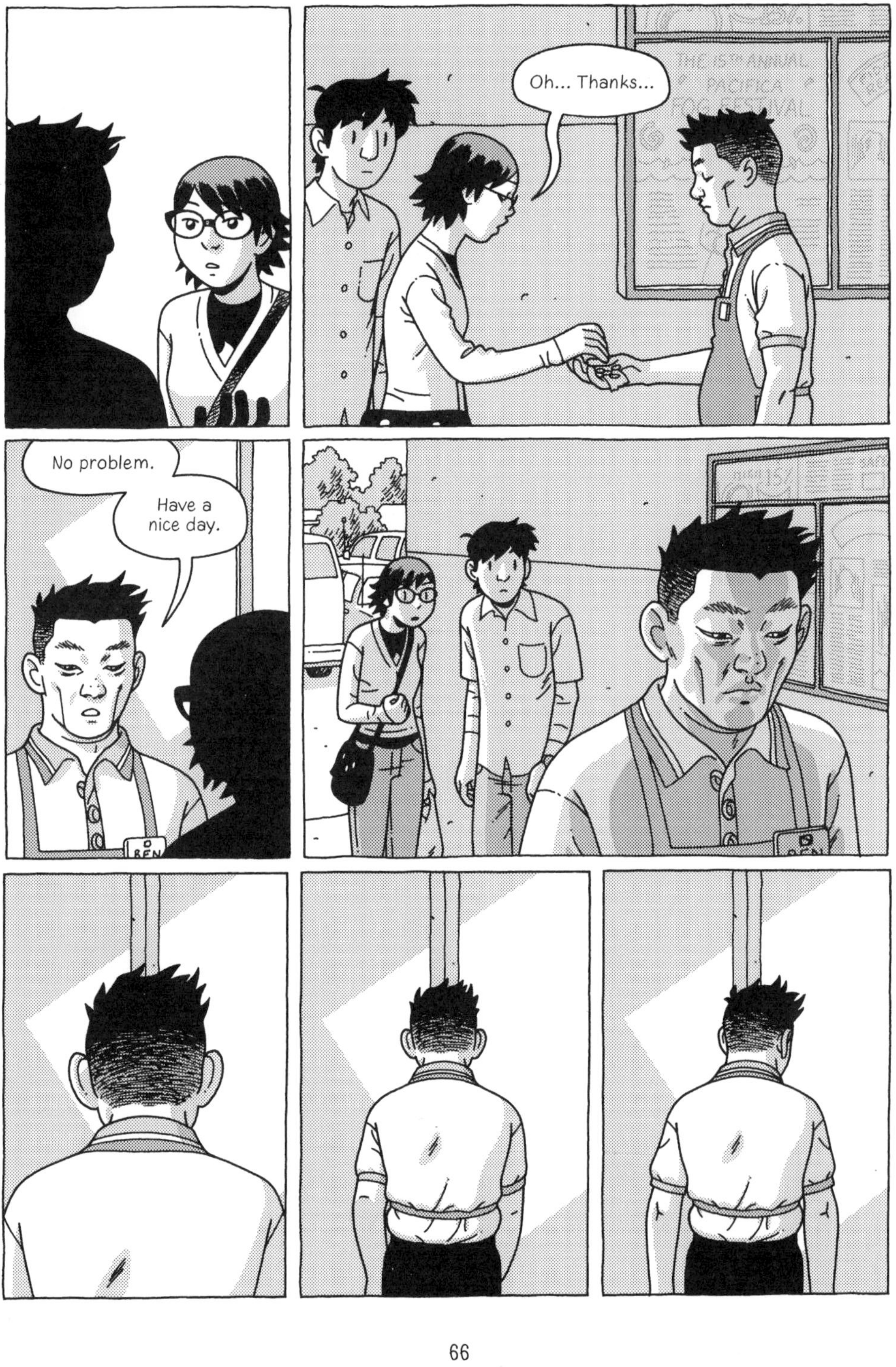
THE 15TH ANNUAL
PACIFICA
FOG FESTIVAL
Oh... Thanks...
No problem.
Have a nice day.

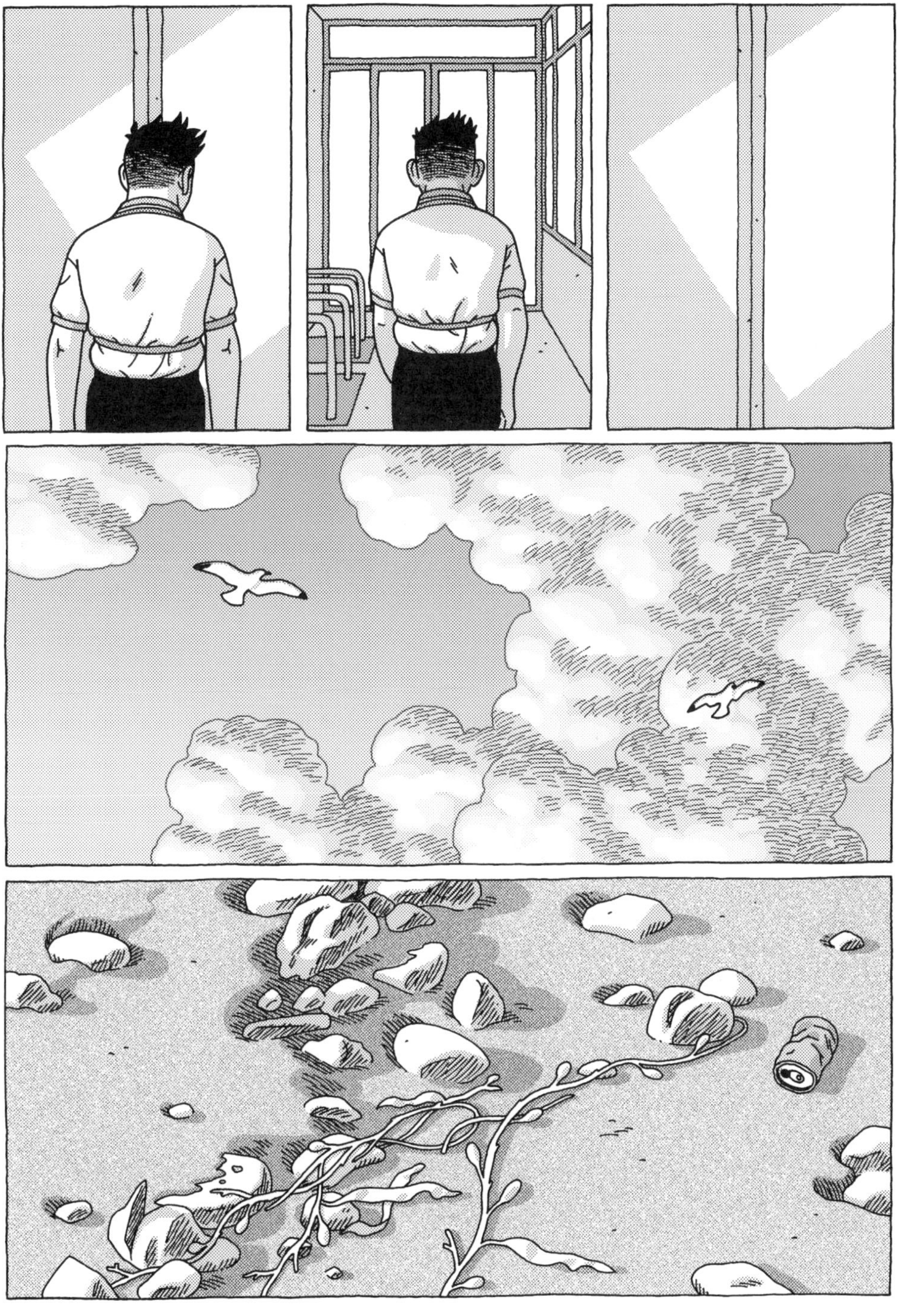

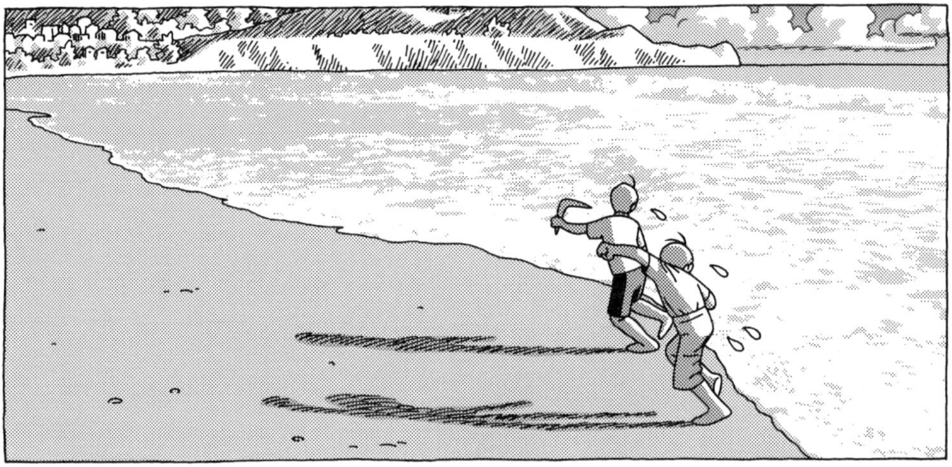

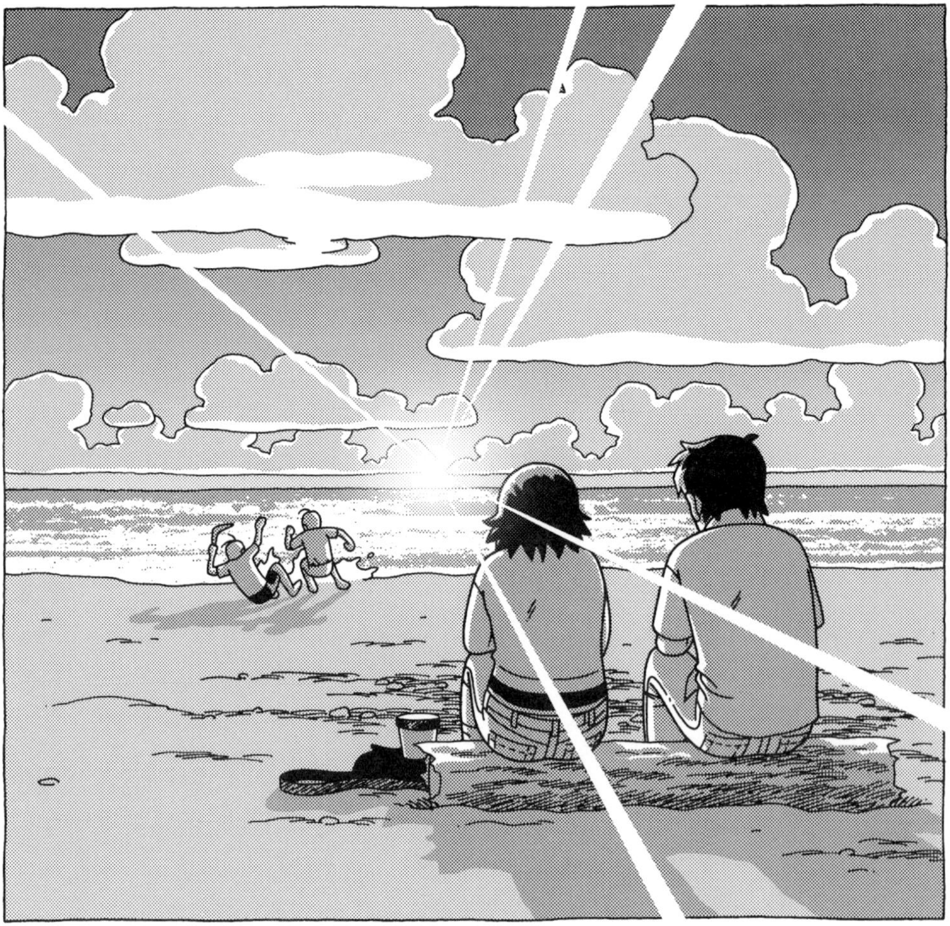

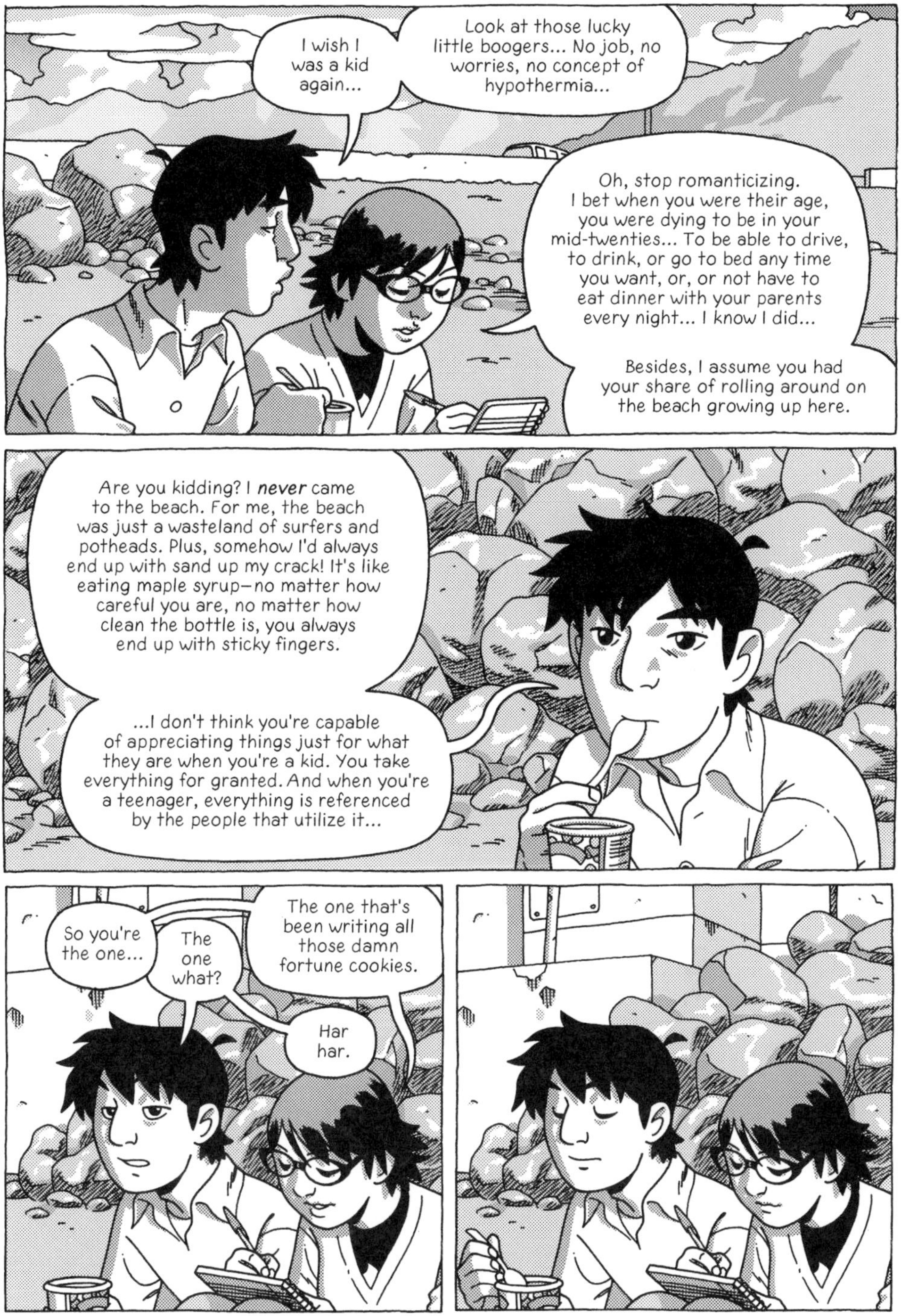
I wish I was a kid again...
Look at those lucky little boogers... No job, no worries, no concept of hypothermia...
Oh, stop romanticizing. I bet when you were their age, you were dying to be in your mid-twenties... To be able to drive, to drink, or go to bed any time you want, or, or not have to eat dinner with your parents every night... I know I did...
Besides, I assume you had your share of rolling around on the beach growing up here.
Are you kidding? I ***never*** came to the beach. For me, the beach was just a wasteland of surfers and potheads. Plus, somehow I'd always end up with sand up my crack! It's like eating maple syrup—no matter how careful you are, no matter how clean the bottle is, you always end up with sticky fingers.
...I don't think you're capable of appreciating things just for what they are when you're a kid. You take everything for granted. And when you're a teenager, everything is referenced by the people that utilize it...
So you're the one...
The one what?
The one that's been writing all those damn fortune cookies.
Har har.

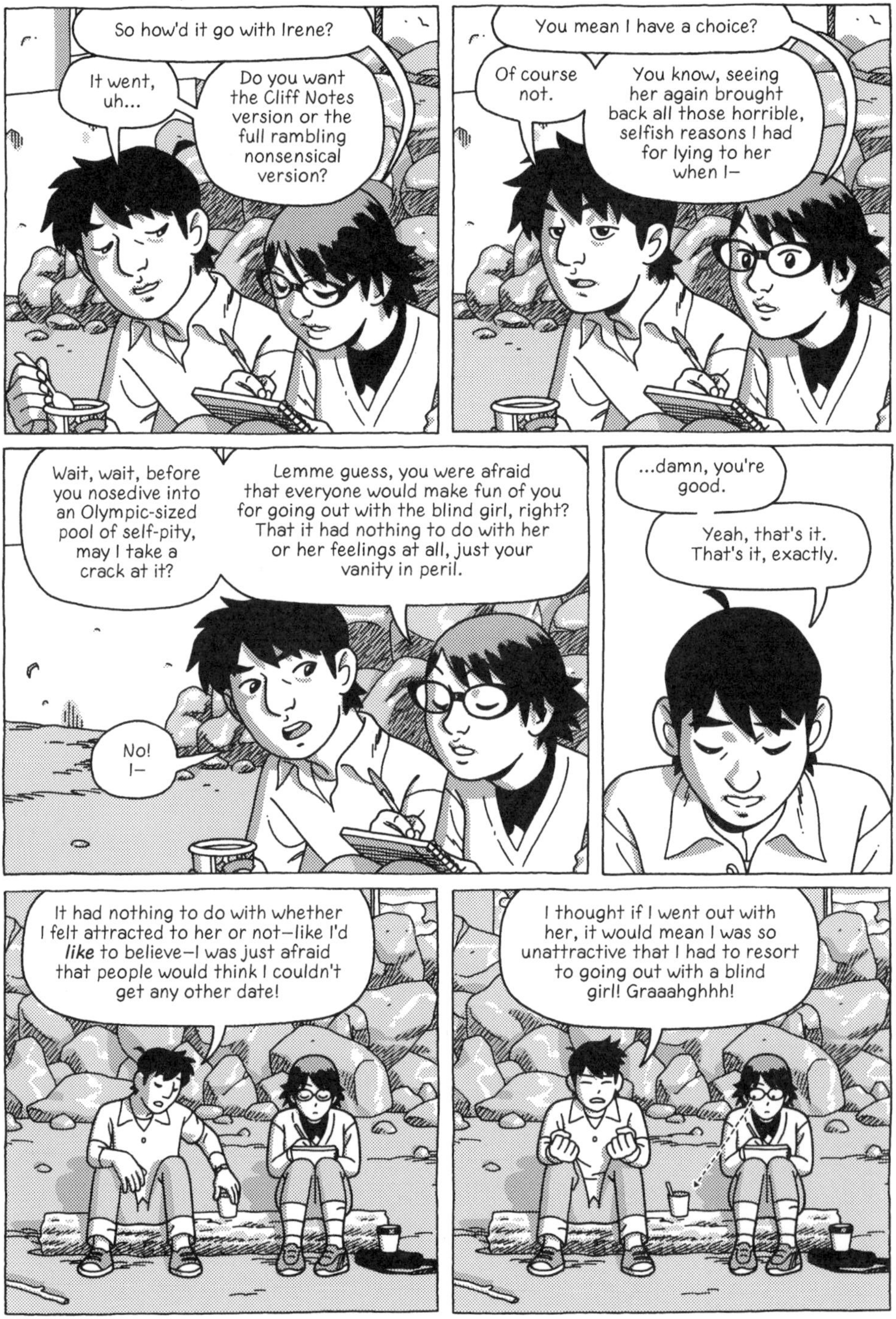
So how'd it go with Irene?
It went, uh...
Do you want the Cliff Notes version or the full rambling nonsensical version?
You mean I have a choice?
Of course not.
You know, seeing her again brought back all those horrible, selfish reasons I had for lying to her when I–
Wait, wait, before you nosedive into an Olympic-sized pool of self-pity, may I take a crack at it?
Lemme guess, you were afraid that everyone would make fun of you for going out with the blind girl, right? That it had nothing to do with her or her feelings at all, just your vanity in peril.
No! I–
...damn, you're good.
Yeah, that's it. That's it, exactly.
It had nothing to do with whether I felt attracted to her or not–like I'd *like* to believe–I was just afraid that people would think I couldn't get any other date!
I thought if I went out with her, it would mean I was so unattractive that I had to resort to going out with a blind girl! Graaahghhh!

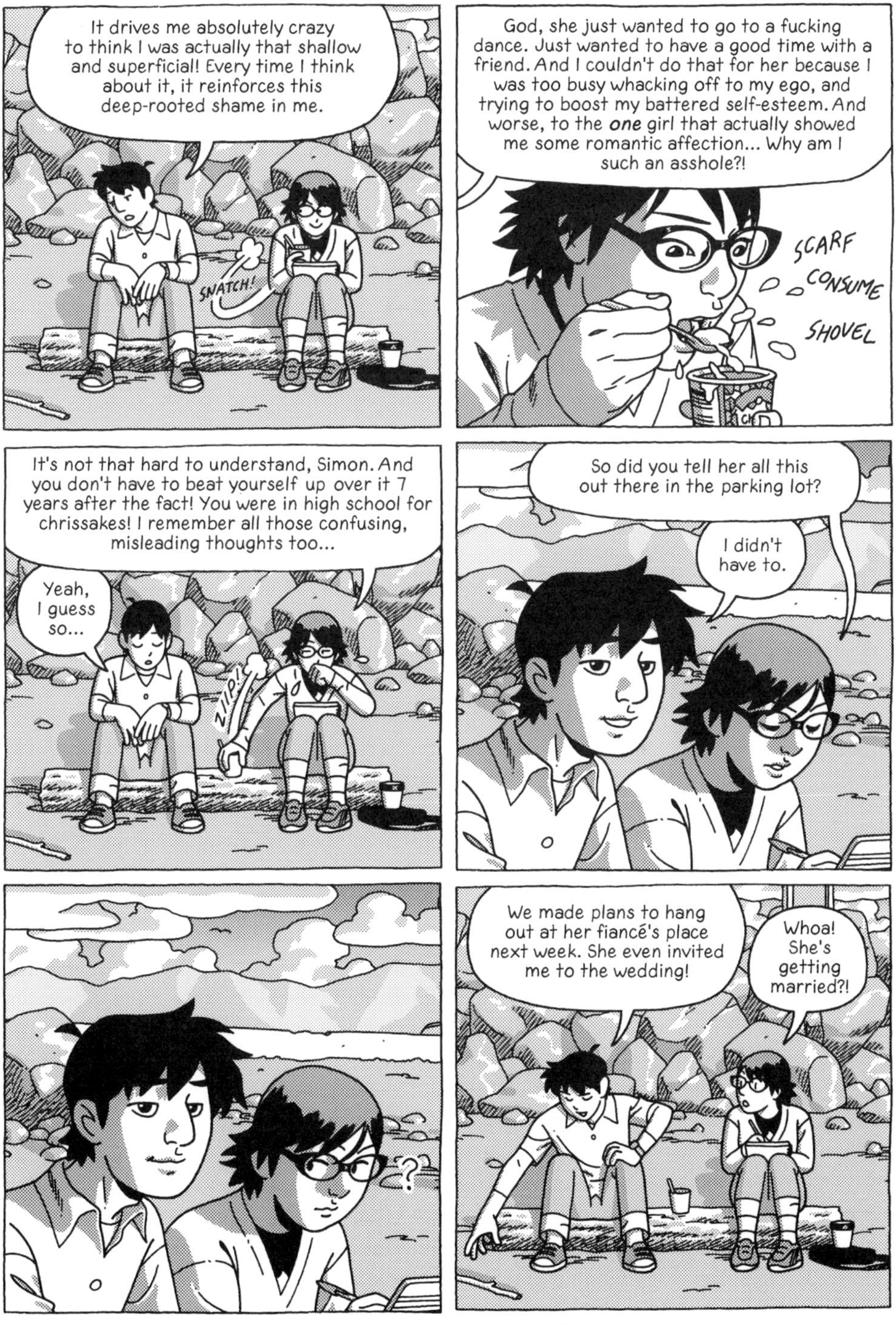
It drives me absolutely crazy to think I was actually that shallow and superficial! Every time I think about it, it reinforces this deep-rooted shame in me.
SNATCH!
God, she just wanted to go to a fucking dance. Just wanted to have a good time with a friend. And I couldn't do that for her because I was too busy whacking off to my ego, and trying to boost my battered self-esteem. And worse, to the *one* girl that actually showed me some romantic affection... Why am I such an asshole?!
SCARF
CONSUME
SHOVEL
It's not that hard to understand, Simon. And you don't have to beat yourself up over it 7 years after the fact! You were in high school for chrissakes! I remember all those confusing, misleading thoughts too...
Yeah, I guess so...
ZIIP!
So did you tell her all this out there in the parking lot?
I didn't have to.
?
We made plans to hang out at her fiancé's place next week. She even invited me to the wedding!
Whoa! She's getting married?!

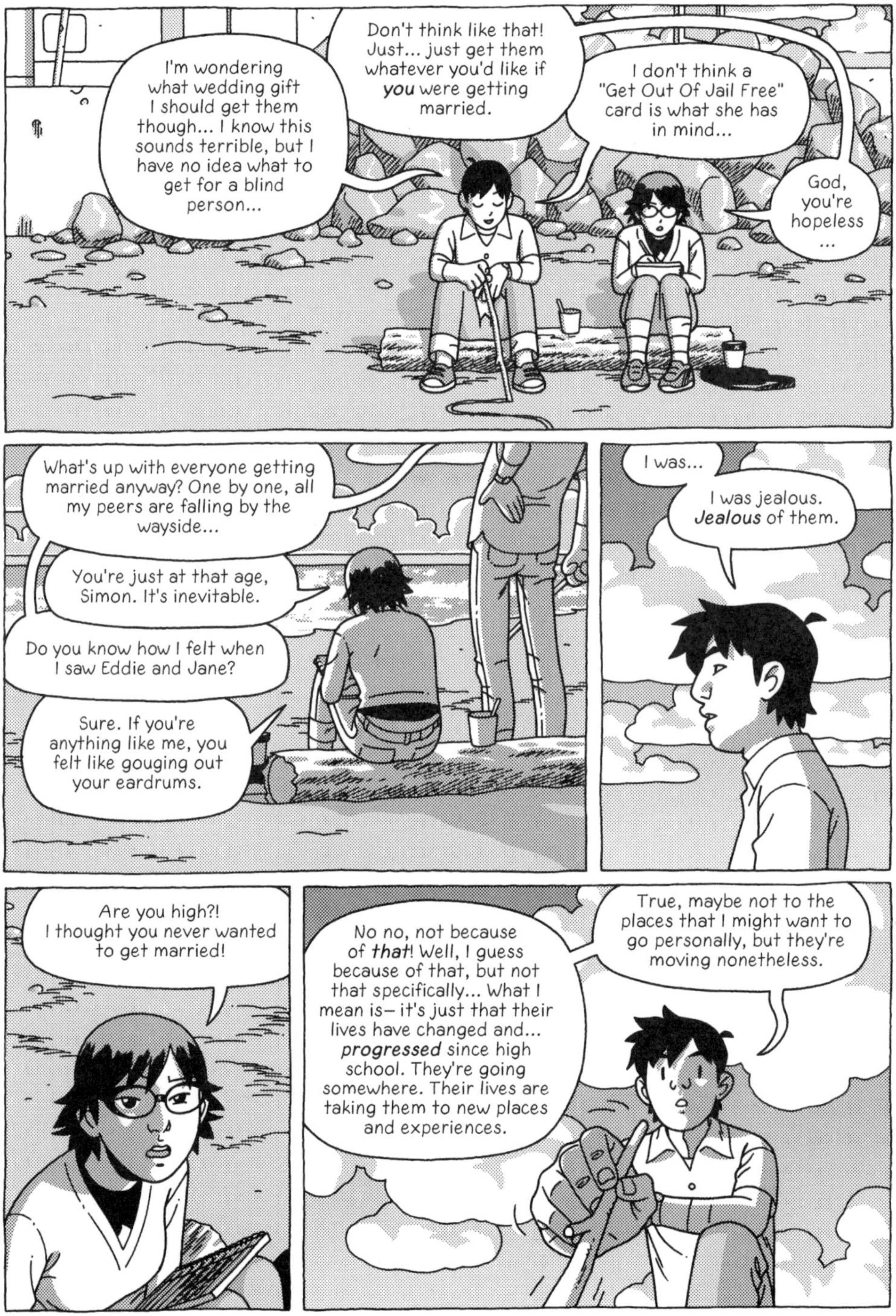
I'm wondering what wedding gift I should get them though... I know this sounds terrible, but I have no idea what to get for a blind person...
Don't think like that! Just... just get them whatever you'd like if *you* were getting married.
I don't think a "Get Out Of Jail Free" card is what she has in mind...
God, you're hopeless ...
What's up with everyone getting married anyway? One by one, all my peers are falling by the wayside...
You're just at that age, Simon. It's inevitable.
Do you know how I felt when I saw Eddie and Jane?
Sure. If you're anything like me, you felt like gouging out your eardrums.
I was...
I was jealous. *Jealous* of them.
Are you high?! I thought you never wanted to get married!
No no, not because of *that*! Well, I guess because of that, but not that specifically... What I mean is— it's just that their lives have changed and... *progressed* since high school. They're going somewhere. Their lives are taking them to new places and experiences.
True, maybe not to the places that I might want to go personally, but they're moving nonetheless.

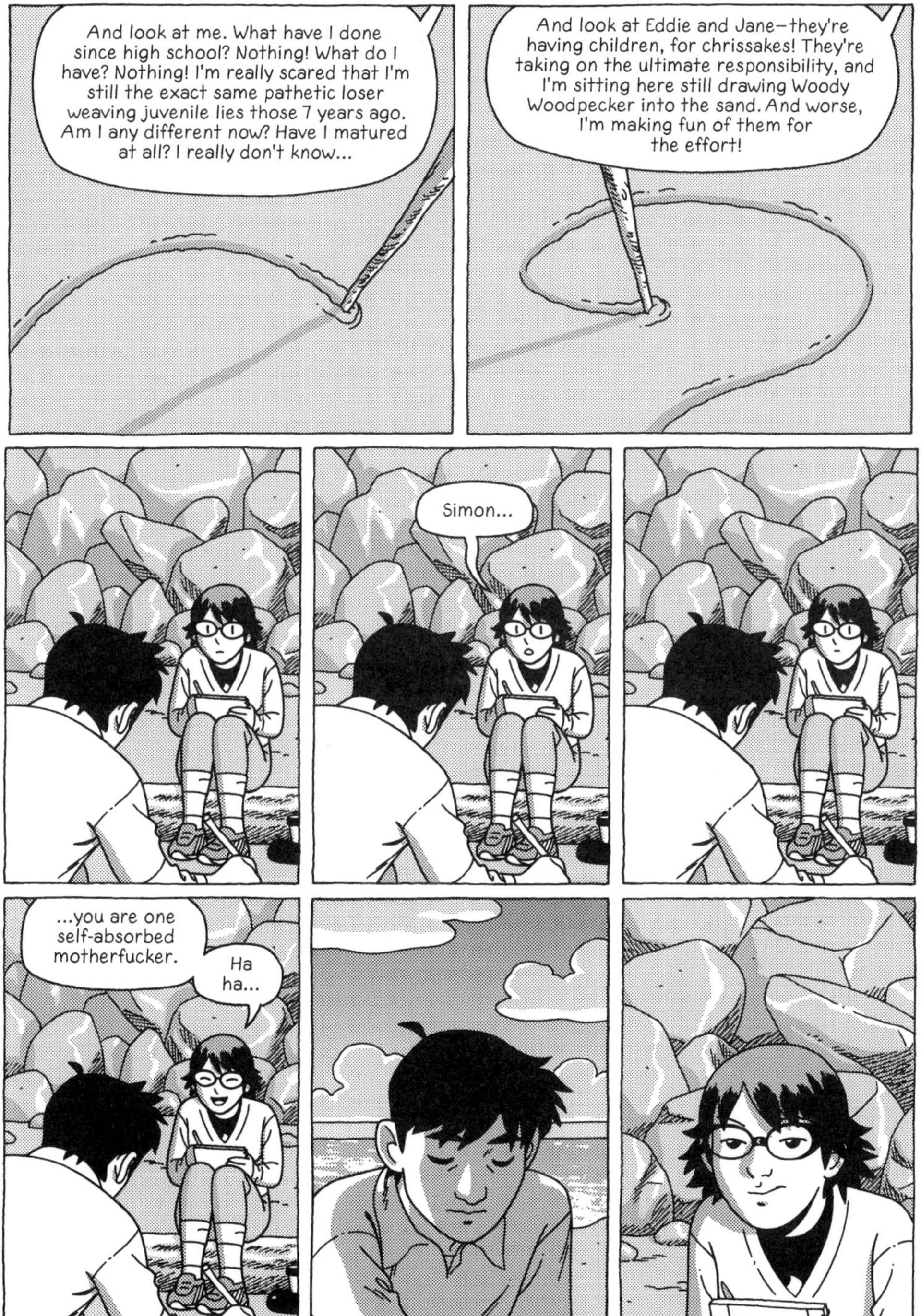
And look at me. What have I done since high school? Nothing! What do I have? Nothing! I'm really scared that I'm still the exact same pathetic loser weaving juvenile lies those 7 years ago. Am I any different now? Have I matured at all? I really don't know...
And look at Eddie and Jane—they're having children, for chrissakes! They're taking on the ultimate responsibility, and I'm sitting here still drawing Woody Woodpecker into the sand. And worse, I'm making fun of them for the effort!
Simon...
...you are one self-absorbed motherfucker.
Ha ha...

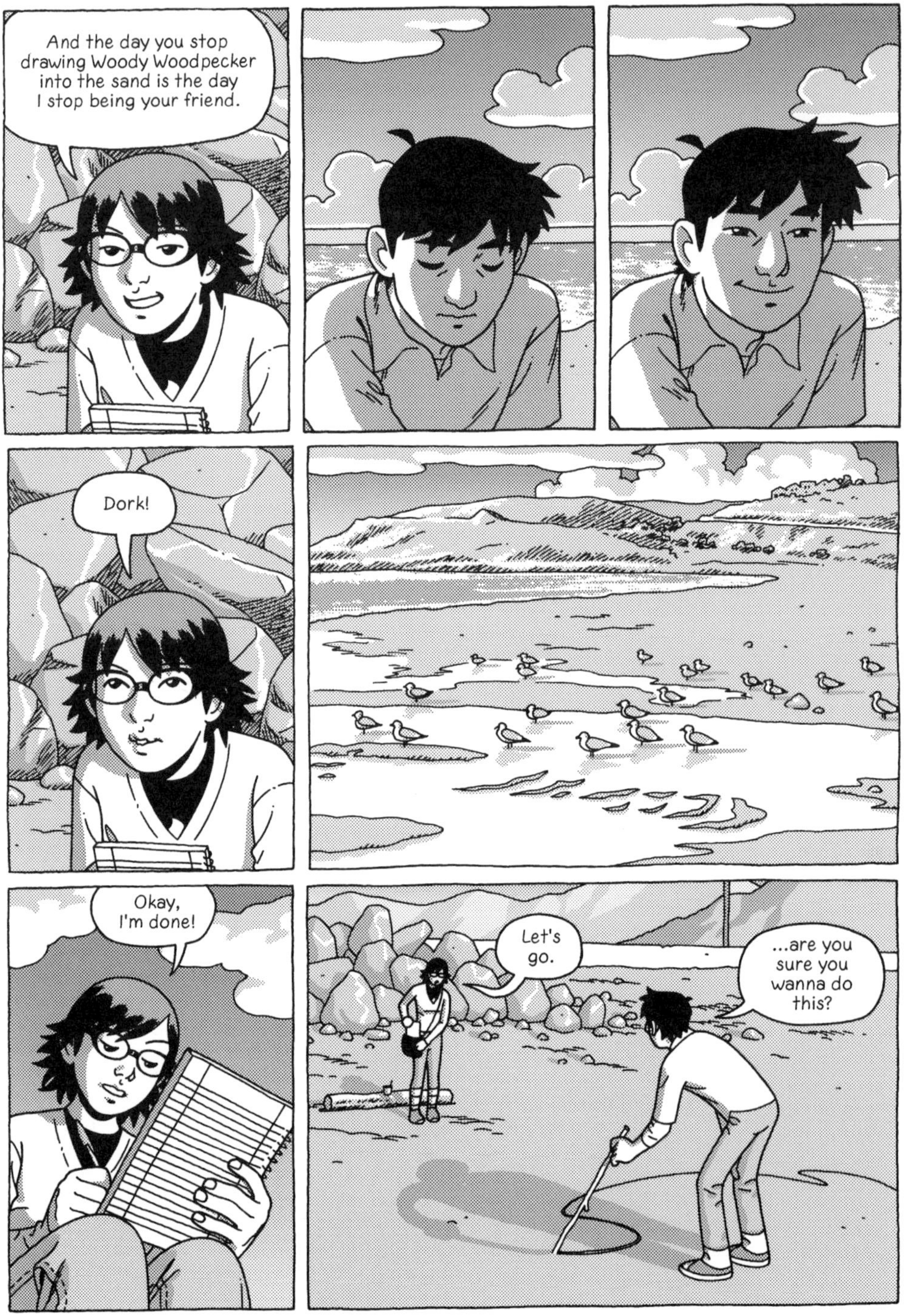

And the day you stop drawing Woody Woodpecker into the sand is the day I stop being your friend.
Dork!
Okay, I'm done!
Let's go.
...are you sure you wanna do this?

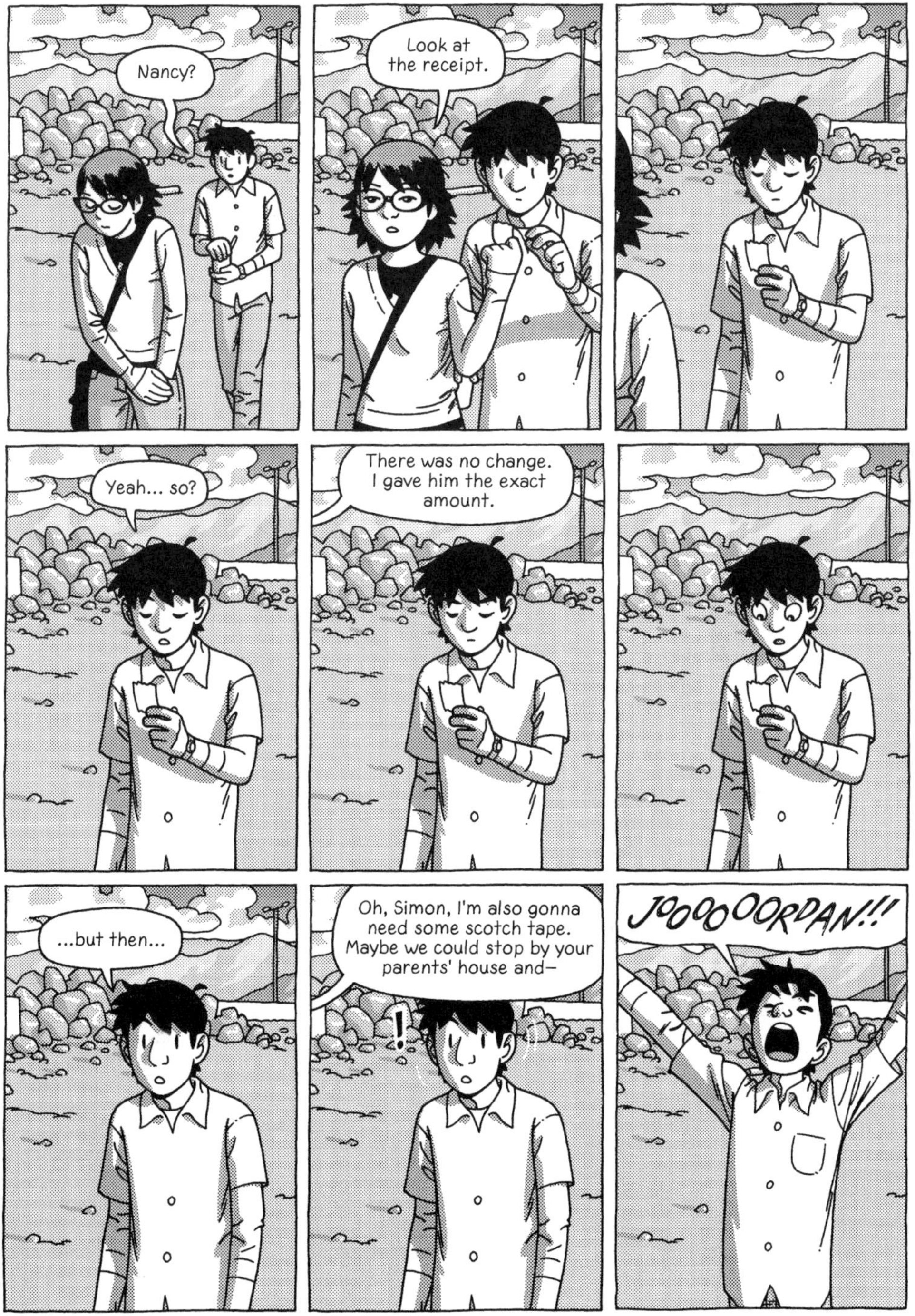
Nancy?
Look at the receipt.
Yeah... so?
There was no change. I gave him the exact amount.
...but then...
Oh, Simon, I'm also gonna need some scotch tape. Maybe we could stop by your parents' house and—
!
JOOOOOORDAN!!!

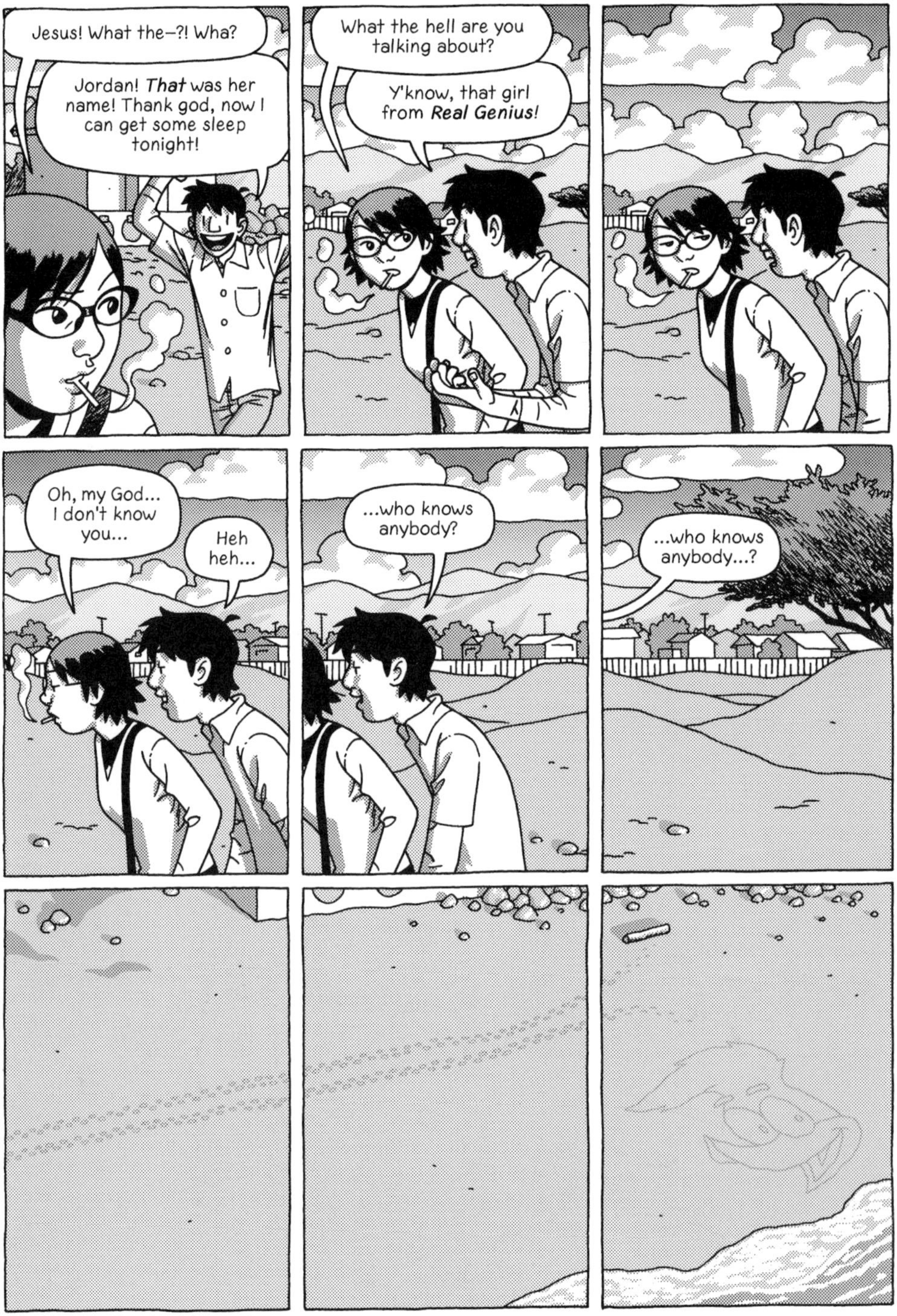

Jesus! What the–?! Wha?
Jordan! *That* was her name! Thank god, now I can get some sleep tonight!
What the hell are you talking about?
Y'know, that girl from **Real Genius**!
Oh, my God... I don't know you...
Heh heh...
...who knows anybody?
...who knows anybody...?

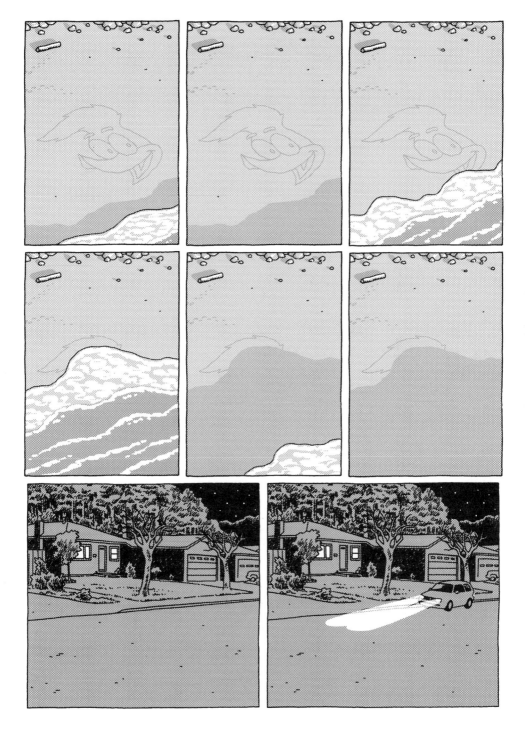

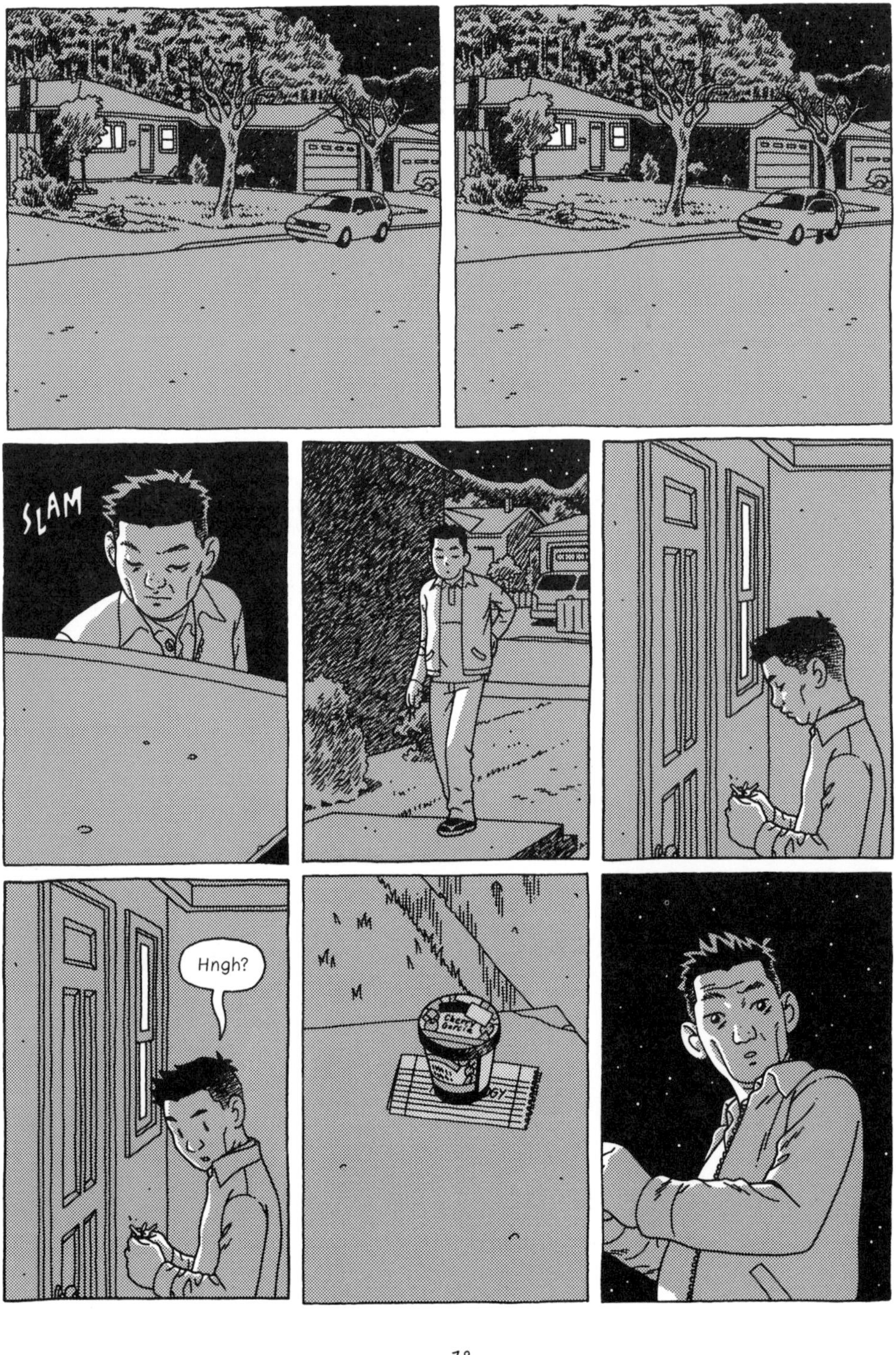
SLAM
Hngh?

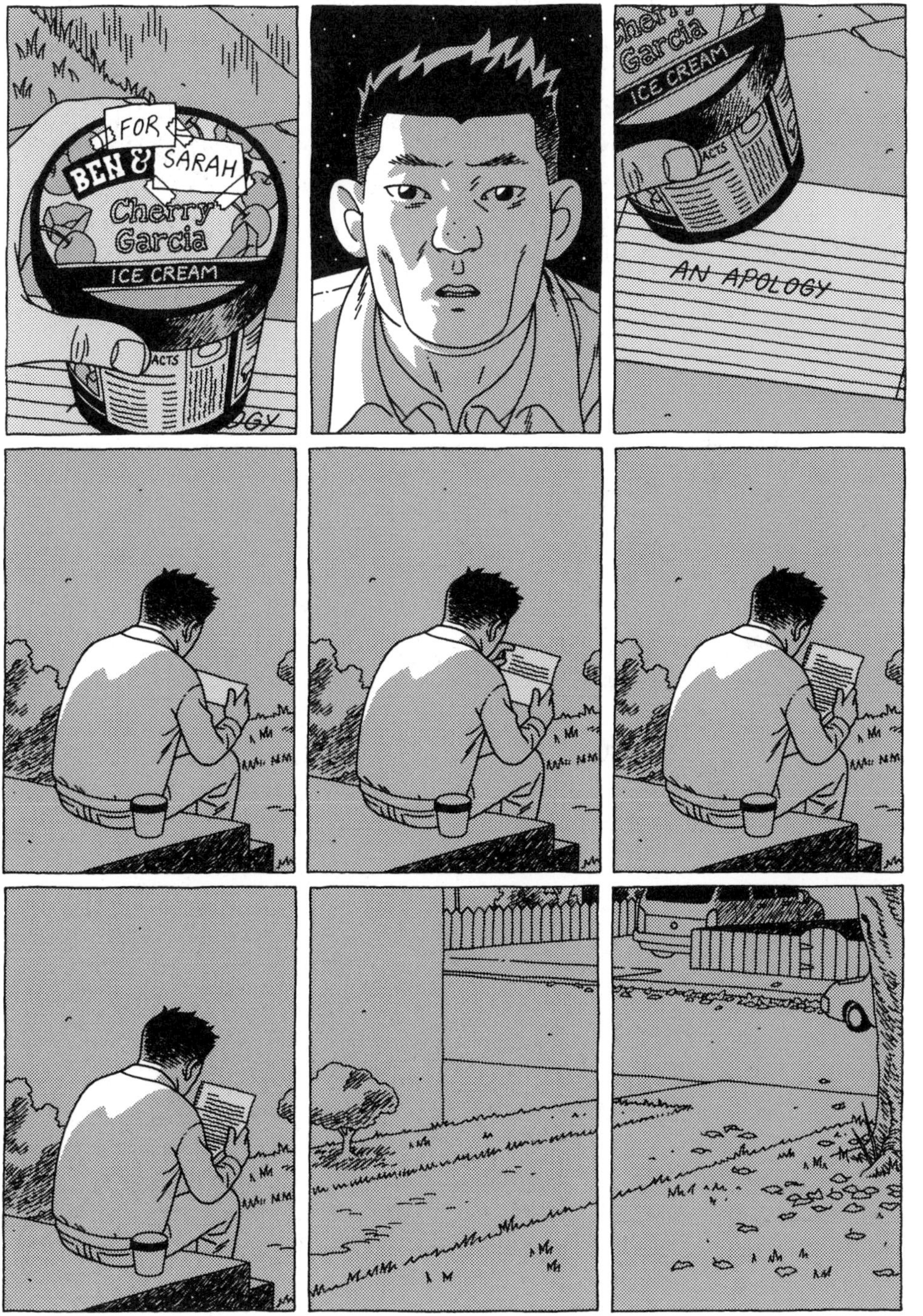
FOR
BEN &
SARAH
Cherry Garcia
ICE CREAM
ACTS
Cherry Garcia
ICE CREAM
ACTS
AN APOLOGY

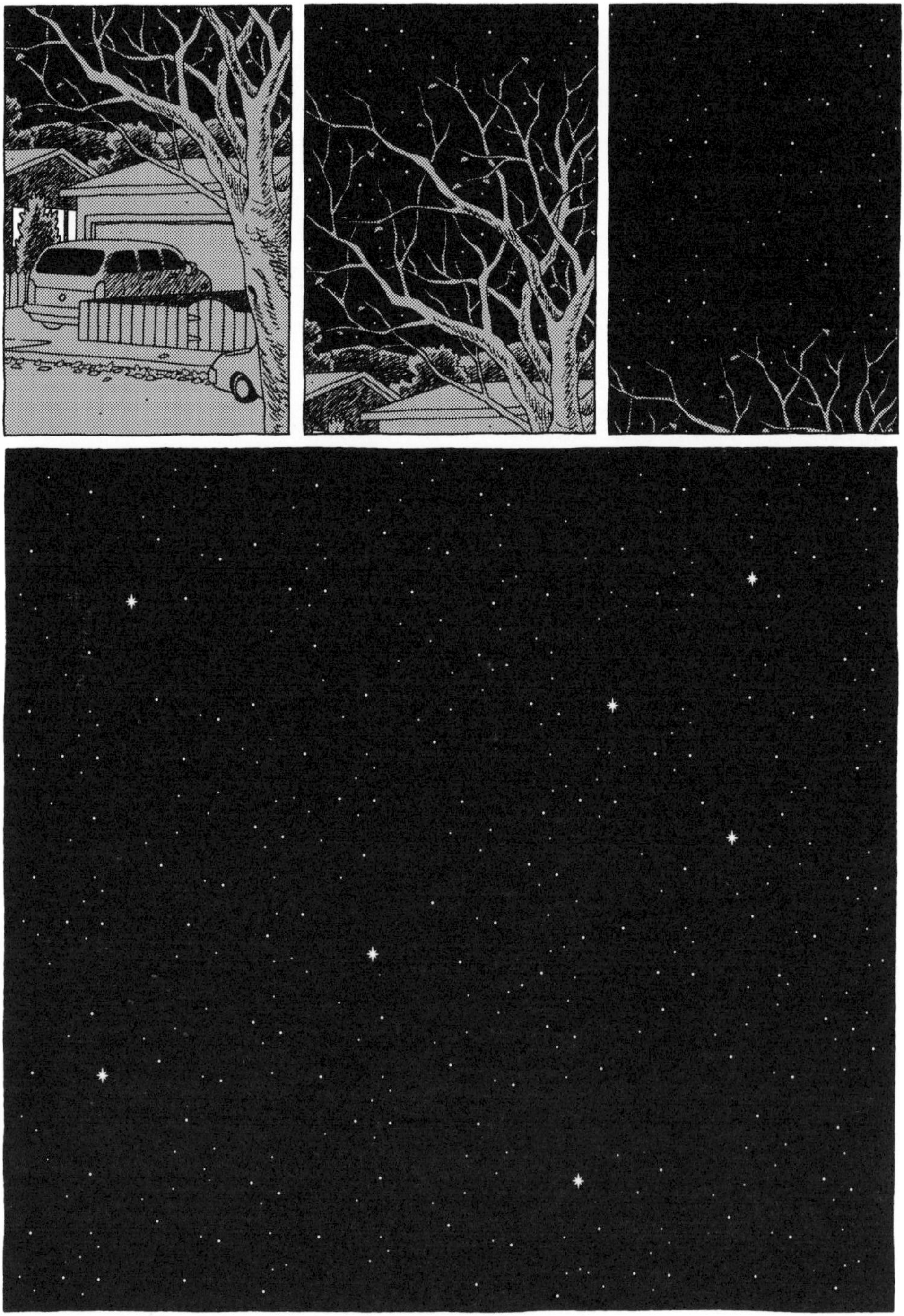

Afterword
by Derek Kirk Kim

It's been eleven years since I started work on *Same Difference*. A lot has changed in that time. Our country has endured three different presidents, an attack of unprecedented tragedy on our shores, a senseless war, and a meltdown in the world's economy. Comics and graphic novels have somehow crawled out of the basement of the publishing world into the daylight of major bookstore chains and become *the* dominant source material for feature films along the way. Since 2000, I have moved eight times—migrating through two countries, three states, and seven different cities—and gone from a part-time English teacher to a full-time cartoonist and writer. I'm pretty sure *Same Difference* had nothing to do with most of this, but that last change in the trajectory of my career can be fully assigned to this modest comics novella.

Same Difference started as a simple 35-page story that ballooned to a slightly less simple story more than double its original length. No matter what I do in the future, *Same Difference* will always be my most significant work. Not the most complex or proficient, and hopefully not the best, but the most significant. Not because of the awards or the professional traction it provided (although these were amazing, unexpected byproducts for which I am immensely grateful), but because of the breakthrough it provided in my artistic evolution.

Same Difference gave me my own voice.

For the first time, the creative process became an honest, organic channeling of myself and not a conscious manipulation of my influences. When I started work on *Same Difference*, the terrible habit of second-guessing the reader and the arrogant expectations of financial reward were finally exorcised from my mind. Please don't misunderstand, I have no illusions about the insignificant place, if any, *Same Difference* holds in the great annals of sequential art or literature, but simply for me, as someone on the artistic path, it was a monumental step forward. Which is why it fills me with such great pride and gratitude to see this beautiful new edition from First Second.

The following pages provide a small peek into the manic creative process that gave birth to *Same Difference*. I hope you enjoy it.

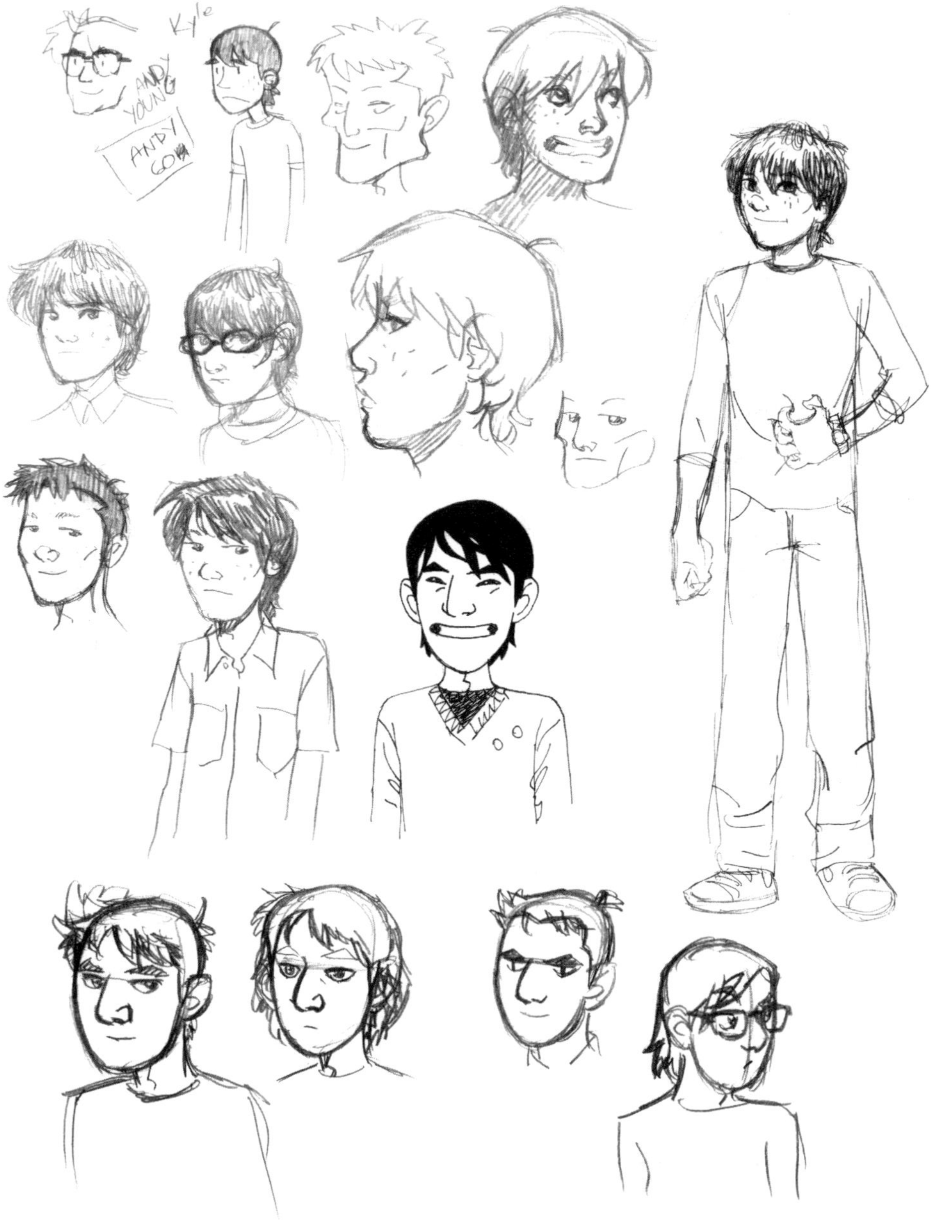
Kyle
ANDY YOUNG
ANDY GO

Simon was the hardest character to nail down visually. As you can see, I went through a number of variations before settling on the design seen in the actual pages. You can also see the other names I toyed with. "Andy Go" eventually went to the central character of *Tune*.

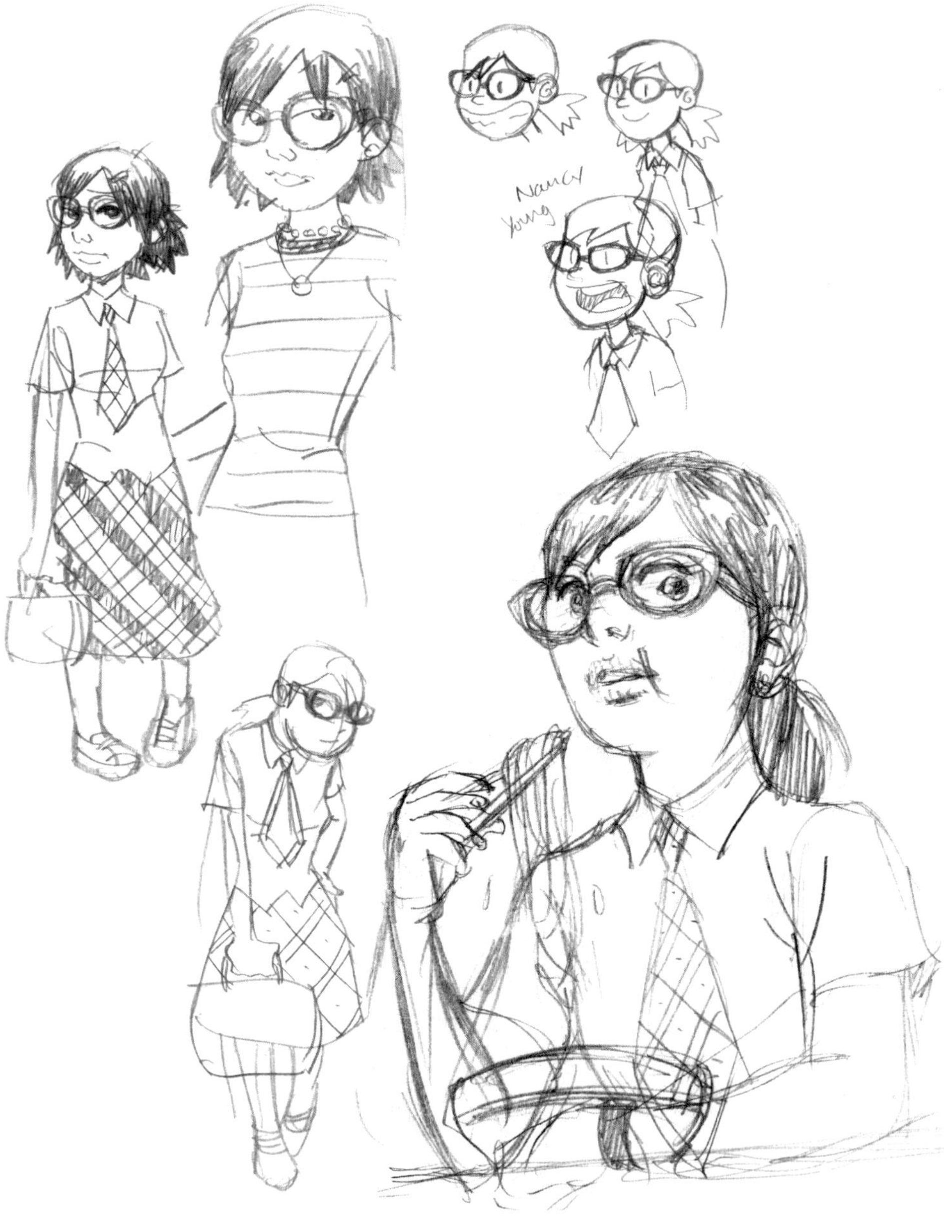
Nancy Young

Nancy was relatively easy to visualize. It really helps when a character is partially based on a friend.

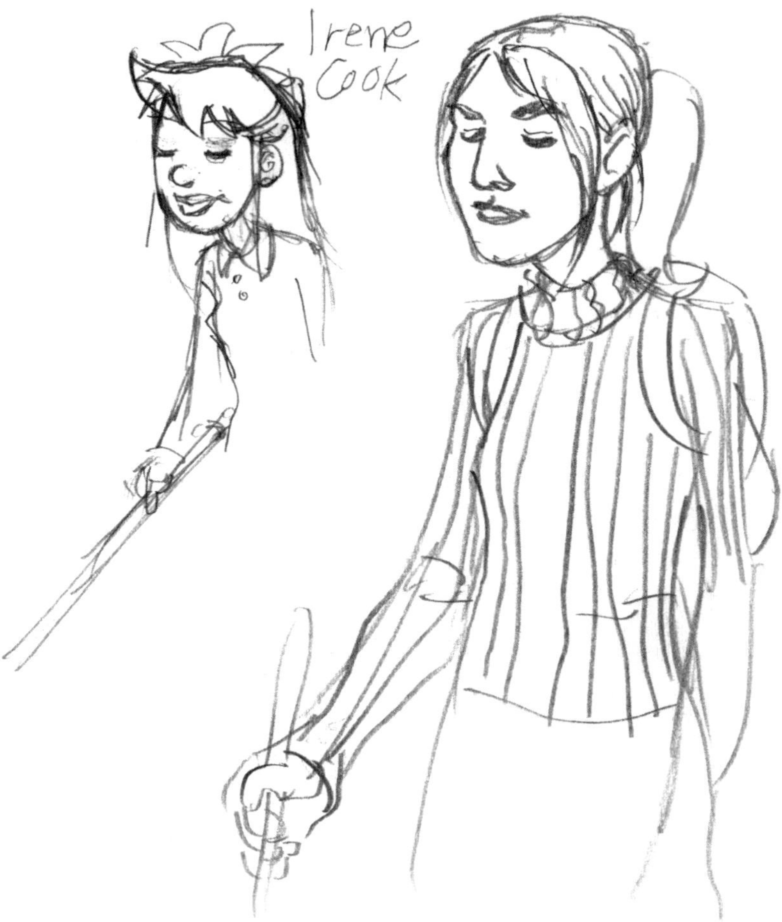
Irene
Cook

Irene sprang to life very quickly. I believe these are the only two sketches of her I did before moving on to the final artwork. Irene was based on a blind high school friend of mine, and, sadly, the story Simon tells in the pho restaurant is lifted directly from my life. In fact, my guilt over that incident was the driving force behind the creation of *Same Difference*.

This was the first fully-inked drawing of Simon and Nancy I put down on paper once their designs were thought to be finalized. But I decided to revamp Simon just before starting actual production. He looked rather forgettable for a central character. I wanted to give him a distinctive look as well as something iconic to draw the reader's attention. Like Charlie Brown's zig-zag shirt or Superman's S-shaped spit curl. I took this idea to the extreme and carved into Simon's face an abstract triangular nose. I actually drew the entire comic this way. It finally took a complaint from a Scott McCloud to shake me back to my senses. That nose just didn't belong in that universe. So I went back and painstakingly redrew every nose on every panel in which Simon appeared, and photoshopped them in.

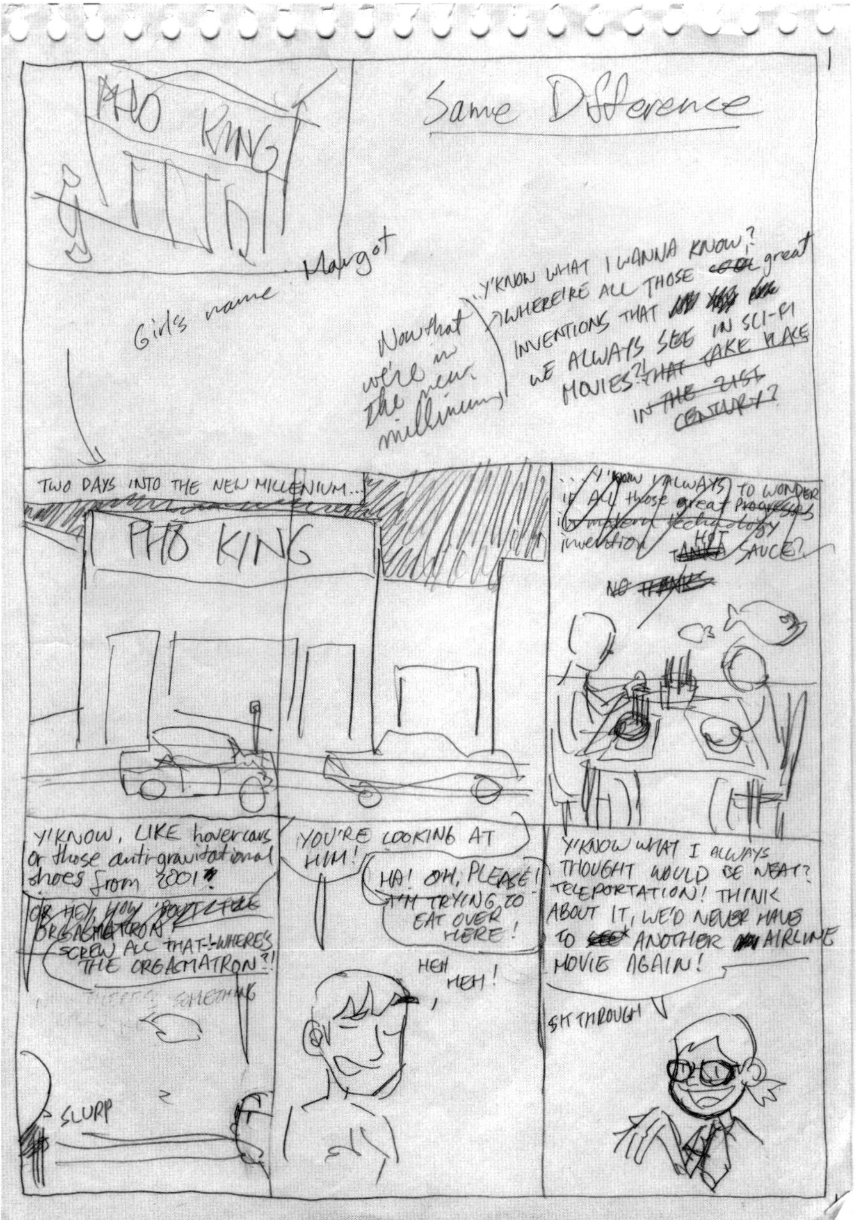

PHO KING
Same Difference
Girl's name Margot
Now that we're in the new millennium
..Y'KNOW WHAT I WANNA KNOW? WHERE'RE ALL THOSE great INVENTIONS THAT WE ALWAYS SEE IN SCI-FI MOVIES?!
TWO DAYS INTO THE NEW MILLENIUM...
PHO KING
HOT SAUCE?
Y'KNOW, LIKE hovercars or those anti-gravitational shoes from 2001!
SCREW ALL THAT--WHERE'S THE ORGASMATRON?!
SLURP
YOU'RE LOOKING AT HIM!
HA! OH, PLEASE! I'M TRYING TO EAT OVER HERE!
HEH HEH!
Y'KNOW WHAT I ALWAYS THOUGHT WOULD BE NEAT? TELEPORTATION! THINK ABOUT IT, WE'D NEVER HAVE TO ANOTHER AIRLINE MOVIE AGAIN!
SIT THROUGH

This is the original thumbnail scrawl of the opening page. Most of *Same Difference* was written this way—totally haphazard and frenetic. Very different from the more structured way I approach writing comics these days.

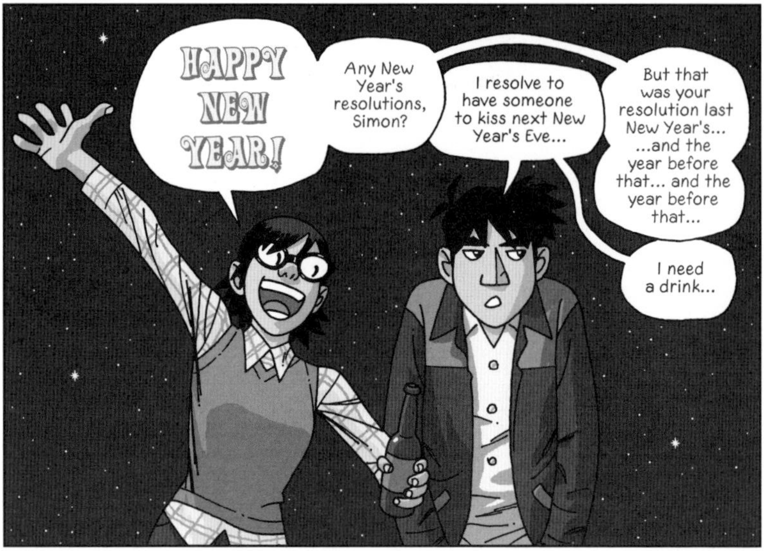
HAPPY NEW YEAR!
Any New Year's resolutions, Simon?
I resolve to have someone to kiss next New Year's Eve...
But that was your resolution last New Year's... ...and the year before that... and the year before that...
I need a drink...

Same Difference was originally serialized at my website, and during its run, Simon and Nancy would often pop up in other little tidbits for the site. This was a New Year's greeting in 2002. There's that silly nose again...

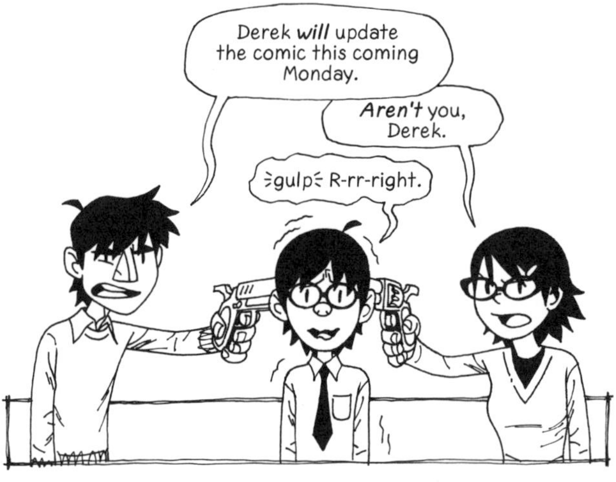
Derek *will* update the comic this coming Monday.
Aren't you, Derek.
gulp R-rr-right.

Simon and Nancy had no patience for a missed update during *Same Difference*'s serialization.

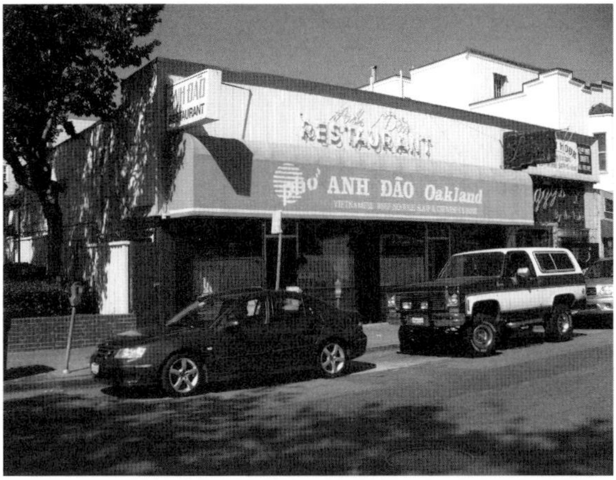
RESTAURANT
PHỞ ANH ĐÀO Oakland

All the locations in *Same Difference* were drawn from real places in the San Francisco Bay Area. The pho restaurant in which the story opens is located near Lake Merritt in Oakland, CA.

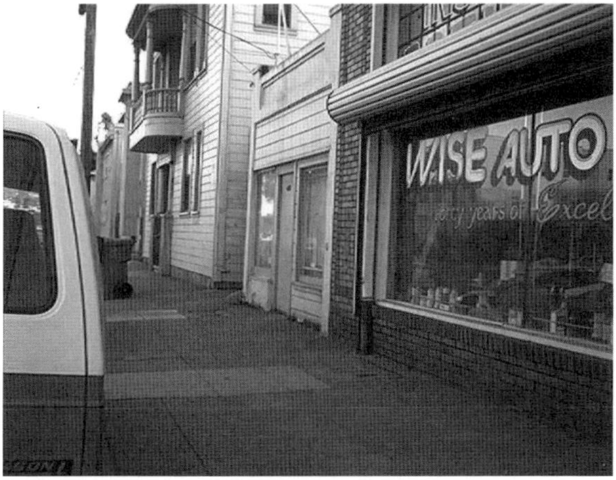
WISE AUTO

Nancy and Dwaine's apartment as seen on page 17. A couple of my friends lived here, and they did have a drum set in the living room.

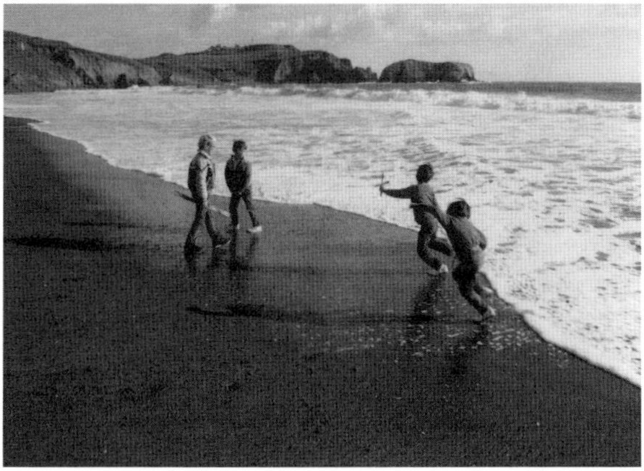

The kids on the beach seen on page 68 are actually my brother and me. This photo was taken by my step father when we were in grade school. My mother was obsessed with putting us in matching clothes, complete with matching bowl haircuts. We're both wearing "I'm a Toys'R'Us Kid!" sweatshirts.

Shots of Linda Mar Beach in Pacifica used for the penultimate scene.